KEY ISSUES IN EDUCATION

Parental choice in education

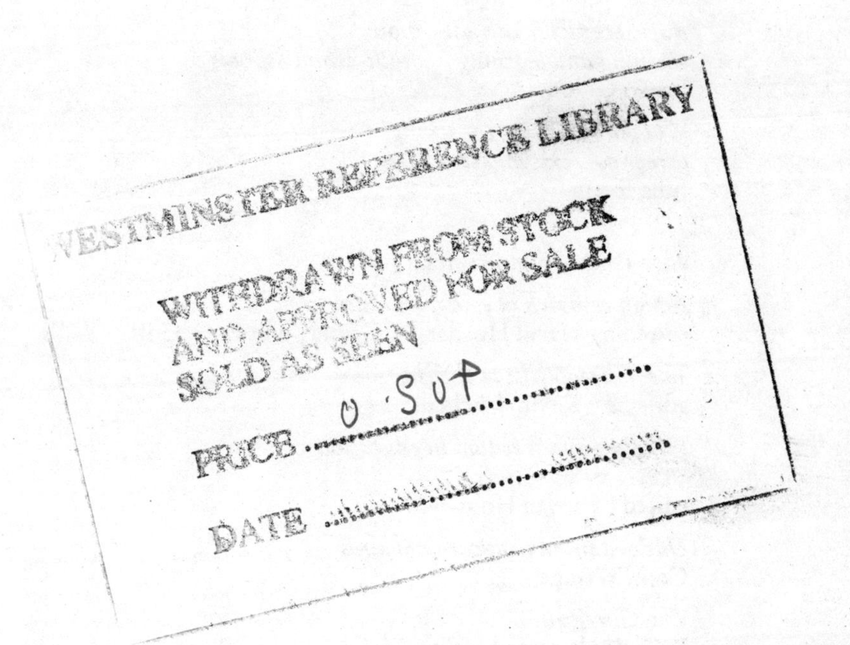

KEY ISSUES IN EDUCATION

The politics of reorganizing schools
Stewart Ranson

Forthcoming in this series

Race, ethnicity and education: teaching and learning in multi-ethnic schools
David Gillborn

Women in primary teaching: career contexts and strategies
Julia Evetts

Also from Unwin Hyman

Action research in classrooms and schools
edited by David Hustler, A. Cassidy and E. C. Cuff

The behaviourist in the classroom
edited by Kevin Wheldall

Equality and freedom in education: a comparative study
edited by Brian Holmes

Understanding educational aims
Colin Wringe

The Curriculum
Brian Holmes and Martin McLean

Examinations
John C. Mathews

KEY ISSUES IN EDUCATION

Series Editor:
Dr Robert Burgess, *University of Warwick*

Parental choice in education

Daphne Johnson
Brunel University

London
UNWIN HYMAN
Boston Sydney Wellington

Published by the Academic Division of
Unwin Hyman Ltd
15/17 Broadwick Street, London W1V 1FP, UK

Unwin Hyman Inc.,
955 Massachusetts Avenue, Cambridge, Mass. 02139, USA

Allen & Unwin (Australia) Ltd,
8 Napier Street, North Sydney, NSW 2060, Australia

Allen & Unwin (New Zealand) Ltd in association with the
Port Nicholson Press Ltd,
Compusales Building, 75 Ghuznee Street, Wellington 1, New Zealand

First published in 1990

British Library Cataloguing in Publication Data

Johnson, Daphne
Parental choice in education. – (Contemporary issues in education)
1. Great Britain. Education. Role of parents
I. Title II. Series
370.1931

ISBN 0-04-370195-7 pbk

Library of Congress Cataloging in Publication Data

Johnson, Daphne
Parental choice in education/Daphne Johnson.
p. cm. — (Key issues in education)
Includes bibliographical references and index.
ISBN 0-04-370195-7 (pbk.)
1. School, Choice of—England. 2. Education—England.
3. Education and state—Great Britain. 4. Education—Great Britain.
I. Title. II. Series.
LB1027.9.J64 1990 90-40193
370'.942—dc20 CIP

Typeset in 10 on 11 point Garamond by Fotographics (Bedford) Ltd
and printed in Great Britain by Billing and Sons Ltd, Worcester

Contents

List of tables

Remembering
Rita McNab
teacher, exemplar and friend

Series editor's preface

Each volume in the *Key Issues in Education* series is designed to provide a concise authoritative guide to a topic of current concern to teachers, researchers and educational policy makers. The books in the series comprise an introduction to some of the key debates in the contemporary practice of education. In particular, each author demonstrates how the social sciences can help us to analyse, explain and understand educational issues. The books in the series review key debates, and the authors complement this material by making detailed reference to their own research, which helps to illustrate the way research evidence in the social sciences and education can contribute to our understanding of educational policy and practice.

All the contributors to this series have extensive experience of their chosen field and have worked with teachers and other educational personnel. The volumes have been written to appeal to students who are intending to become teachers, working teachers who seek to familiarize themselves with new research and research evidence, as well as social scientists who are engaged in the study of education. Each author seeks to make educational research and debate accessible to those engaged in the practice of education. At the end of each volume there is a short guide to further reading for those who wish to pursue the topic in greater depth. The series provides a comprehensive guide to contemporary issues in education and demonstrates the importance of social science research for understanding educational practice.

Parents and parental choice are key elements of education policy. Indeed, recent legislation in the UK has placed parents at the centre of the educational stage. In this respect, Daphne Johnson's book is very timely. She examines research evidence on parents and parental choice in state and independent schools. Her book is therefore an important resource in contemporary educational discussion and debate for those actively engaged in the education service as participants and researchers as well as lay persons.

Robert Burgess
University of Warwick

Author's preface

Since the passing of the 1988 Education Reform Act, this book on parental choice in education has been addressing a moving target. Policy has been articulated, and practice is taking over. Parental choice is indeed a contemporary issue in education. Throughout 1988 and 1989, the subject has rarely been absent from the columns of the national and educational press. Even before the Reform Act reached the statute book, parents at Dewsbury in West Yorkshire were pressing for the right of open enrolment. Since the Act, the saga of grant-maintained ballots and applications has been unending, although relatively few schools have, at the time of writing, actually acquired grant-maintained status.

Parental choice, however, is not just a short-lived craze. Its pros and cons have been debated by educationalists, economists and philosophers since the earliest days of publicly funded education. It is an issue in which many deeply held values are embroiled. Some of these have found expression in research reports as well as in political pamphlets and manifestos.

Parental choice in education looks at the subject in the round, in the light of the 1988 Education Reform Act and its immediate aftermath. To make a large subject less unwieldy, I have focused my discussion on education in England, and the opportunities it offers for parental choice. However some major pieces of research into parental choice have been carried out in Scotland, and these are discussed with other research in chapter 3. Parental choice in special education is not dealt with in this book. This important subject must be explored elsewhere.

I am glad to acknowledge the help of all those who have contributed in any way to the preparation of *Parental choice in education*, especially Michael Adler, Hugh Boulter, Richard Cunningham, Geoffrey Duncan, John Fitz, John Morgan, Andrew Turner and Geoff Whitty. Robert Burgess has been a supportive and perceptive editor, and I am grateful to Jane Harris-Matthews for her patience and encouragement. All errors are my own.

Daphne Johnson
October 1989

Chapter 1

Thinking about parental choice

'Parental choice is a key element of our policy'.
Kenneth Baker, Secretary of State for Education[1],

Are parents being used by government to bring about politically motivated changes in education? Or are parents in fact the people best fitted to make new choices about their children's schools? Whatever the motivation for their involvement, parents are now at centre stage of the educational scene. When a government which has legislated for a major act of educational reform (the 1988 Education Reform Act) affirms that parental choice is a key element of policy, this means more than any manifesto of intention. One way or another, parents now have a new part to play in education. How has this come about?

Although parents have a new and central importance in the final decade of the twentieth century, their responsibility for children's learning has long been acknowledged.[2] The introduction of compulsory schooling, however, imposed on parents a largely acquiescent role in their children's education. Their task was to make sure their children attended school, then leave the teachers free to operate in their own professional sphere.

Being responsible for sending children to school was not likely to earn parents a place on the central political agenda. School attendance has been, and remains, a problem in some families and some areas, but it has not engaged the attention of central government for many years. Attendance monitoring and enforcement has been a local matter, sometimes almost entirely a school matter (Johnson *et al.*, 1980; Bird *et al.*, 1981). Parents who fulfil the requirement to send their children to school are taken for granted. Those who fail to do so are handled as a local nuisance rather than as a seedbed of political rebellion.[3]

For the first three or four decades of the twentieth century parents were tacitly expected to keep their own distance from their children's schools, but some new expectations arose following the 1939–45 war. The 1944 Education Act made mention of the 'wishes' of parents concerning their children's schooling.[4] However, this was a very small step on the road to parental choice. The wishes parents were expected to express concerned the religious education of their children, linked to the introduction of the 'dual system' of voluntary and local authority schools (see chapter 2). Far more pressing for central government, in the late 1940s and early 1950s, was the 'roofs over heads' requirement (1944 Education Act, s.8), entailing a massive expansion in school provision so as to accommodate the increasing school-age population, whose school years were also about to lengthen (Middleton and Weitzman, 1976; Gosden, 1983).

Although parents remained politically insignificant, educationalists began to look at them in a slightly different way. Research into the potentially beneficial effects of parents on children's learning began to seep through into teacher awareness (Davis, 1950; Fraser, 1959; Floud, 1961; Douglas, 1964). Parents were gradually encouraged to draw closer to the school, to learn from teachers and reinforce their work with the child (Midwinter, 1972). For many educationalists, that is still the preferred role for parents.

Although the 1944 Education Act made only minimal reference to the wishes of parents, it did provide a way for some parents to make their presence felt at central government level. Parents who did not approve of the local authority's choice of school for their child could appeal to the secretary of state.[5] To begin with, this tactic was only rarely used, but as standards of education and styles of secondary and primary schooling became matters of popular controversy in the 1960s and 1970s, the number of appeals to the secretary of state greatly increased.[6] The political and administrative embarrassment caused by these numerous claims contributed to the growing feeling of both major political parties that parents should have some more local forum of appeal about choice of school. New mechanisms for the expression and implementation of parental choice featured both in the Labour government's (abortive) 1978 Education Bill, and in the Conservative government's first major new move on education, the 1980 Education Act. A policy to strengthen the position of parents of school pupils was in any case very much in line with the consumerist emphasis of the first and subsequent Thatcher administrations.

Certainly throughout the 1980s, during the passage of the 1980 and 1986 Education Acts, culminating in the 1988 Education Reform Act, parents were on the political as well as the educational agenda. Policies were put forward, and legislation enacted them, giving parents a far more central role to play in their children's education. The rights of parents to choose their child's school, to enrol their children at the school up to the limits of its physical capacity, and to propose changes in the status of a school by acting collectively to 'opt out' of local authority control, petitioning the secretary of state for grant-maintained status, were central tenets of education reform as set out in the 1988 Act. Parental choice is now an important consideration in all plans made by schools and education authorities.

What are teachers to make of all this? As professionals they cannot ignore a situation so relevant to their working lives. Bearing in mind the main arguments for and against the involvement of parents in choosing children's schools, they will want to check these against the policy as they see it in practice. And if parents are going to choose, what is the range of choice now available? What are the mechanisms through which choice can be exercised? Teachers may want to do some research of their own into how parental choice works out, as policy is put into practice around them. What research has already been done? In this book the groundwork for exploring all these issues is laid down, and further reading suggested. We begin by examining views on what say parents should have in their children's education.

Compulsory education: the 'no choice' policy

Why should parents have to send their children to school at all? Why should they not be free to make their own decisions about what, if anything, their children need to learn? There are four main arguments in favour of formal schooling for all children. They are:

- the neighbourhood effects argument
- the protection of minors argument

- the social cohesion argument
- the equality argument

All these arguments advocate some kind of government intervention in education, so as to minimize the differences between families.

NEIGHBOURHOOD EFFECTS ARGUMENT

This argument can be applied generally to all aspects of common life, not just education. The actions of any one person have an effect on other members of society. Friedman (1962) points out that the action of one individual may impose significant costs on other individuals for which it is not feasible to make him compensate them. Society may also *benefit* from the actions of an individual, with significant gains to his or her neighbours. When applied to education, the neighbourhood effect is usually assessed as a significant gain. 'The education of my child contributes to your welfare by promoting a stable and democratic society' (Friedman, 1962, p. 86). The inference is that for a stable and democratic society to flourish, some minimum degree of literacy and knowledge is needed by most citizens. Because society as a whole would suffer if individual families declined to educate their children in this way, schooling should be compulsory.

Friedman supports the neighbourhood effects argument but is also strongly in favour of the retention of parental choice of particular schools. He suggests that although government may need to be the channel for society's financial support of universal schooling, there is no reason why education should actually be delivered through publicly provided schools. Instead of setting up schools, government could use taxes to fund privately provided schools, or to make a cash or voucher grant to families sending their children to such schools. (Rowley [1969] sets out the economic arguments for these and other alternatives.)

PROTECTION OF MINORS ARGUMENT

This argument for compulsory schooling suggests that children, who are not legally responsible for their own well-being and behaviour, need protection and guidance beyond that which may be provided by the immediate family. Compulsory schooling provides such protection.

Where the protection of minors is concerned, compulsory schooling is usually equated with state-provided schools. Within this frame of reference, parents are defined as passive, if not positively neglectful, concerning their children's education. They are not seen as having individual or knowledgeable views about the type of education from which their children will best profit nor about where such education might be found. They need a school 'laid on'. However this approach can be criticized as paternalistic,[7] taking parents to be as much in need of guidance and 'spoon-feeding' as their under-age children.

SOCIAL COHESION ARGUMENT

The notion of 'social cohesion' is that if people hold a number of values in common, society holds together and can work in harmony. Education, especially state-provided education, provides a way of exposing all citizens to the same value system. Exactly what the desirable common value system would comprise is not usually (and perhaps cannot be) spelt out, but its effect would be to stimulate consideration for others and minimize competitive self-interest. Crosland (1964, p. 46) points out that these ethical aims are embedded in certain socialist doctrines. Tawney (1931) made the alleged *lack* of shared value systems a focus of his strong attack on the continuing existence of private schools alongside state-provided education:

> A special system of schools, reserved for children whose parents have larger bank accounts than their neighbours . . . is at once an educational monstrosity and a grave national misfortune. It is educationally vicious, since to mix with companions from homes of different types is an important part of the education of the young. It is socially disastrous, for it does more than any other single cause, except capitalism itself, to perpetuate the division of the nation into classes of which one is almost unintelligible to the other.
> (Tawney, 1931, p. 145)

EQUALITY ARGUMENT

While the neighbourhood effects, the protection of minors and even the social cohesion arguments are relatively subdued and theoretical arguments in the late twentieth century, all more or less disposed of by the existence of free public education for over one hundred years, the equality argument is still a matter of current debate. Equality is one of the basic philosophic ideals. Warnock (1975) contends that equality and justice are related concepts, both implying behaviour according to a rule. If you say that 'everyone has an equal right to education' you need a further specifying rule about *what* education each has a right to. However, if you say that 'everyone has a right to equal education' this is itself a specifying rule, suggesting everyone has the right to the *same* education. This egalitarian notion of the same education for everyone has been an influential idea, but does not take account of the differing personal resources which people bring to their education, and which may affect its outcome. Warnock suggests that in its pure form egalitarianism is an unacceptable and unattractive idea, implying uniformity between people as well as between the way they are treated. More usually, the equal right to education has been interpreted as an equal *opportunity* for education. Warnock sees this as two different rights: 'the right to a certain amount of ['needed'] education and the chance or opportunity to get more ['desired'] education' (Warnock, 1975, p. 4). The equality argument has been kept alive by a debate as to where the line should be drawn between these two rights.

Basic 'needed' education could be said to have been taken care of by the legislation for compulsory free elementary education at the end of the nineteenth century. But since some children received additional 'desired' secondary education, in schools paid for by their parents, and other children found a sponsored entry to secondary education through competitive examination and local authority funding, the next target for those promoting the equality argument became 'secondary education for all'. The 1944 Education Act (s.7) ostensibly met this requirement by recasting the statutory system of public education into 'three progressive stages to be known as primary education, secondary education and further education', and by extending compulsory schooling first to fifteen and then sixteen years of age. Moreover, there would be no fee for admission to any school or college maintained by a local educational authority (LEA).

The 1944 Act did not specify in what kinds of schools secondary education should be provided, but most LEAs selectively allocated pupils to secondary modern and grammar schools, or in a few cases to secondary technical schools. However, in a famous phrase of the period, the schools did not achieve 'parity of esteem' (Banks, 1955) and this provided new fuel for the equality argument. While young people were acknowledged to need differing emphases in their secondary education, arguments were put forward for meeting those differing needs in an egalitarian setting, the comprehensive secondary school (Pedley, 1956, 1963).

As comprehensive secondary schooling became more widespread, attention turned to the continuing coexistence of secondary schools outside the LEA remit, where fees could still be charged: the independent schools and the direct grant schools, which received funding from central government. Could equality in education be said to exist as long as there was an alternative group of schools, access to which depended on ability to pay? For the direct grant schools the equality argument became an irresistible force. All public money to these schools was phased out from 1975 (Direct Grant Grammar Schools (Cessation of Grant) Regulations, S/I 1975/1198) and the buying of LEA places in certain independent schools was made more difficult by the 1976 Education Act.[8] However the fully independent schools, their number now augmented by the majority of the 'ex-direct grant' schools,[9] proved an immovable object, for the time being at least (see chapter 2). Public and private fee-paying education continue to coexist, and this coexistence still provides a strong focus for the equality argument.[10]

However, there are others. Local authorities devote differing resources to education, and manage those resources in differing ways.[11] Children bring not only differing abilities but also differing cultural capital to their education[12] and even in a non-fee-paying education system the financial and practical support which some parents give their children's schools can make a noticeable difference to amenities. The particular problems that schools face are not equal either. In some areas the transient presence of mobile families with children spending brief periods on the roll of a school, or the presence on roll of many children whose mother tongue is not English, provides a challenge which other schools may not face. Even the ability to give all children the opportunity of five days a week schooling from the earliest admission age may be threatened in some extreme circumstances.[13]

Policies for equality in education have achieved a great deal, but the world is an unequal place and many of its inequalities are reflected in the nation's schools.[14] Will parental choice widen those inequalities?

The pros and cons of parental choice of school

> The polarisation of opinion [about plans for parental choice] reflects a division on very deeply held values, involving beliefs about the proper division of authority between the state and the family, beliefs about the danger to social cohesion of deviant doctrines, beliefs about the relative abilities of professionals and their clients to decide what is best, and beliefs in the importance of maintaining the existing institutional order.
>
> (Coleman, in Coons and Sugarman, 1978, p. xi)

Arguments in favour of parental choice tend to be based on an individualist view of the world. They are not new arguments. In the eighteenth century, as the idea of some government support for existing schools began to be debated, an active role for parents in arranging their children's education was urged by Adam Smith (1776) and the American philosopher Tom Paine (1792). Paine held that public money should be distributed to families to buy their children's education (rather than that schools themselves should receive endowments). Parents receiving this money should be under a parental duty to pay for adequate education. Smith believed that the market force of parental choice of school would stimulate schools to more efficient teaching, thus contributing to the creation of prosperity. In the nineteenth century the philosopher J. S. Mill (1859) also looked at the educational implications of a commitment to individualism. He urged a combination of parental choice and, where necessary, state subsidy of tuition fees. However, both in the United States and in Britain, in the later nineteenth century the drive for compulsory public education pushed into abeyance these libertarian arguments for parental choice.[15] Although parental choice and government-provided education are not wholly incompatible ideas, there is an inherent tension between them, a tension to which we shall return.

To speak of the exercise of parental *choice* in education implies that some form or forms of education exist between which choices can be made. For children to be educated in accordance with 'the wishes of their parents' may mean that the parents themselves educate their children – and the 1944 Education Act does not rule this out.[16] But to legislate for choice assumes that the parent is looking beyond the home and taking a critical look at forms of education which already exist. Advocates of parental choice are not usually in the 'de-schooling' camp.[17] They tend to accept the reality of an institutionalised professional contribution to children's education, but to require a greater diversity of forms, or more ready access to the range of institutions which exist.

PARENTS AS EXPERTS ON THEIR OWN CHILDREN

Although parental choice in education has, as we have seen, become a prominent educational policy theme in Britain, the case for parental choice was first revived in the United States. Coons and Sugarman, two lawyers from the University of California, Berkeley, became interested in parent–education relations while handling litigation about school finance and governance. They make a case for parental choice on the grounds that, in the late twentieth century, no social consensus exists over what are the proper goals and means for education.

> In its vision of individual human perfection, America is a virtual menagerie. Despite a superficial sameness born of an industrial economy, there is no American ethic or, if there is, it is passing. Dedicated work and dedicated consumption remain a central theme but no longer dominate the mass of personal aspirations; the work ethic competes with challenging cultural, religious, and artistic world views for the loyalty of individuals. This pluralism of individual views about what it is that makes for a fully human life has its impact on education.
>
> (Coons and Sugarman, 1978, p. 1)

In this pluralist society, Coons and Sugarman contend, parents' sensitivity to, knowledge of and partiality for their children are the best equipment for making educational choices.

> In its unique opportunity to listen and to know and in its special personal concern for the child, the family is his (*sic*) most promising champion and a fit senior partner of a decision-making team.
>
> (Coons and Sugarman, 1978, p. 53)

Coons and Sugarman do not suggest that parents should be left to make isolated and unassisted choices. The availability of professional help would be an important component of a family choice plan, and families would be expected to use it. But the professional monopoly of decision-making about children and their schooling would be broken. 'Because of the scale and anonymity of schools . . . no professional speaks – or is even capable of speaking – for many individual children' (Coons and Sugarman, 1978, p. 52).

In a later return to the same theme, Sugarman (1980) sets out clearly his reasons why family insights have the edge over professional appraisals. He claims that families listen to the child's voice, have detailed knowledge about their children and care about their children. He further argues that since families have to make all other important decisions about their child, they should also be trusted to make decisions about education.

In summary, the case made for parental choice in the USA by Coons and Sugarman is that there is no social consensus on what education should consist of; the scale and anonymity of the school system, and the process of allocation of children to schools, leave much to be desired; families care about and know the needs of their own children, and are best fitted to influence decisions about their schooling. Are these ideas also applicable to Britain? They are not the arguments for parental choice which have been most strongly promoted here.

PARENTS' RIGHTS

In Britain, the debate about parental choice has been more politicized, focusing not so much on family relationships as on competing ideologies of individualism and collectivism. Those who favour parental choice base their case not on the *skills* of the parent in identifying the child's need, but rather on the *right* of the parent to guide his or her child through the schooling years without overriding regard to decisions made by other parents, or to collective arrangements made for education by the state. Under twentieth-century arrangements for state education, it is claimed, 'parent-consumers' are 'locked' into the system (Seldon, 1986). Parents are in a tactically weak position, faced with a bilateral monopoly, which Seldon describes as 'a dominant government buyer (proximately local government, ultimately central government)' confronting 'a dominant supplier (the teachers organised in unions)'. Any dispute between these parties is, he claims, likely to be decided 'by arbitrary conditions that have little to do with the well-being of pupils or the opinion of parents' (Seldon, 1986, p. 3). Moreover the state system of education, like any other public bureaucracy[18] is geared for expansion rather than contraction, with the costs being borne by 'large numbers of unsuspecting, widely dispersed parent taxpayers most of whom have no control, or knowledge, of how their money is being spent'. (Seldon, 1986, p. 77). Accountability, as well as sensitivity to individual need, is at issue here.[19]

For Seldon and others (West, 1982; Flew, 1983) the key to this locked system is a voucher, which would allow parents to compare schools and move between them (Seldon, 1986, p. 1). The *capacity* of these parents to make such choices is not argued for. Rather, it is taken for granted that they are equally as capable as those now using the private schools who already exercise such a choice. Indeed, the incapacity of parents to make educational choices, whilst it may be respectably argued by professionals, would require tactful handling by any political party. As Flew points out:

> It is one thing to talk about irresponsible, ill-informed working-class parents . . . quite another to say anything of the sort on the doorstep canvassing for [their] votes . . .'
>
> (Flew, quoted in Seldon, 1986, p. 33)

Collectivist views of society do not entirely rule out parental choice but give it much less prominence. Their first priority is equality of opportunity in education. The Labour Party's *Charter for Pupils and Parents* (1985) suggested that 'building on the achievements of the primary school, . . . the introduction of a fully comprehensive school system, together with the phasing out of fee paying in the private education sector, are the only ways of providing equal opportunities for all' (Labour Party, 1985, p. 5). In the context of such an egalitarian and comprehensive system, parents would have 'the right to express a preference for a school they wish their child to attend, and to receive special consideration if they live near the school'. More important, however, would be parents 'partnership' role with the school, their involvement in its work, and their 'substantial representation on the governing body running the school' (Labour Party, 1985, p. 2). Parents are seen as capable of working closely with professionals, provided the professionals have time and training to enter such a partnership (Radice, 1986).

PARENTS AS KNOWLEDGEABLE CONSUMERS

Some individualists, on the other hand, while considering parents well equipped to make an initial choice of school, expect choice to follow careful enquiries about the school and its teachers. Thereafter, the school entrusted with the child would be left to exercise its professional educational skills. The Hillgate Group, on the right wing of the individualist school of thought, in 1986 published a radical manifesto for education (Hillgate Group, 1986). An important feature of the manifesto's proposals was that parental choice would channel public money to the chosen schools. Parents should be 'free to send their children to any school that is willing to admit them'. They should also have a right to know the policy and outlook of the school, and to have all information 'relevant to a parent's choice'. The schools themselves, however, would have a right to control their own admissions. Headteachers would have 'control – within broad and nationally approved guidelines – over what is taught in their schools, and over the appointment of teachers' (Hillgate Group, 1986, p. 14). Schools would be subject to inspection by HMI (whose procedures, criteria and accountability would have been reviewed). In this scenario, parents' relationship with professionals would not so much be one of partnership and involvement, but rather one of prior appraisal, after which they entrusted the child to professional guidance through the schooling years.

PARENTAL CHOICE AS UNDEMOCRATIC

The notion of the parent as a knowledgeable consumer buying an education 'package' is strongly opposed by Baron *et al.* (1981), who see parental choice as essentially undemocratic. Consumers can 'shop around' but have little or no control over what is offered. The main lines in the schools supermarket, these authors suggest, are determined 'not by an active participating politics of schooling, but by measures of "necessary" scarcity' (Baron *et al.*, 1981, p. 252).

Moreover, the ideal of parental choice de-politicizes the rights and interests of a range of citizens, in that it is based not on *actual* parents and their wishes, but on some misleading abstraction of the 'ordinary' parent. All parents are assumed to be motivated by *petit bourgeois* aspirations. Treating parents as a group united in seeking a better life for their child plays down the varying interests and differing social power of people with children of school age. Stressing parental choice has the effect of homogenizing the parental community and disguising gross inequalities. The interests of a homgenized community in education are defined 'not in terms of political citizenship and democratic participation', but according to a 'mean and self-regarding version of "parental choice" ' (Baron *et al.*, 1981, p. 242).

Another democratic objection which Baron *et al.* make to the parental choice idea is its failure to address the rights of children.[20] They claim that, by sanctifying parenthood as the ownership of children, parental choice treats children not as present or future citizens with equal rights to education but as adjuncts to families which, in their real social existences, have markedly unequal resources and powers. The idea of parental choice also defines children as essentially passive and subject to adult authority. Schooling offered and accepted on these lines can provoke real conflicts between adults and children (Baron *et al.*, 1981, p. 258).

PLANNING VERSUS CHOICE

Most of the arguments for and against parental choice so far discussed have debated the right and the capacity of parents to influence their children's schooling in various ways. But there is also a 'planning' argument which rejects parental choice as leading to administrative inefficiency. In a time of falling rolls, ideas about parental choice are in competition with the need to rationalize local provision of schooling. Administrators' criteria may be to retain an even geographical spread of school places, or to retain schools where resources have recently been invested in buildings or amenities. Parental choice may however be based on very different criteria. Allowing schools to wax or wane according to their popularity, demonstrated through open enrolment, could unbalance local provision, perhaps denying future generations of children access to a local school: once closed, schools can rarely be re-opened. Ranson (1990) firmly takes the view that it is necessarily the responsibility of the LEA, in a time of falling rolls, to ensure that each school has an adequate and balanced intake. Open parental choice inhibits planning and is contrary to the public interest. While notions of the market-place have their value, they have limited applicability to schools. Here, consumer choice would *change* the product available, in that a greatly enlarged or diminished school would not be the same school. Because of this, consumerism in education cannot achieve its objectives of giving parents access to the school of their choice, and increasing the accountability of schools. Citizenship, rather than consumerism, should be the guide. Ranson advocates 'a charter for justice; an enabling authority (the LEA), institutions in partnership with the public and an active citizenship involved in and shaping public choice' (Ranson, 1990, p. 122).

Implications of the 1988 Education Reform Act for parental choice

Which of all the foregoing ideas and arguments has the 1988 Act taken on board? We conclude this chapter by examining some sections of the Act and relating them to the discussion so far.[21]

The Education Reform Act introduces, among other things, the local management of schools (LMS). This is an important innovation in school funding, which merits a book of its own. Local authorities, headteachers and governors have much work to do in grappling with the scheme. For our purposes, it is sufficient to note the significant point that about 75 per cent of each school's budget will be calculated on a per capita basis. Funding will be directly linked to pupil numbers, and these numbers will depend on parents choosing the school.

So far as parental choice itself is concerned, the heart of the Act is sections 26 to 32 on admissions to county and voluntary schools. We shall examine these first, before going on to consider the parts of the Act which relate to the national curriculum (ss 1–25), grant-maintained schools (ss 52–104), and city colleges (s. 105). All these sections of the Act have substantial implications for the availability and exercise of parental choice. Our purpose is to see which of the many current ideas about parental choice these sections of the Act appear to embody, and which ideas were invoked in opposition to or support of the Act during the consultative phase which preceded legislation.[22]

ADMISSIONS TO COUNTY AND VOLUNTARY SCHOOLS

Government claims that the 1988 Act provides for 'a significant enhancement of the ability of parents to secure the admission of their children to the school they prefer' (DES, 1988, para. 1). The Act follows on, and occasionally amends, steps already taken in this direction by the 1980 and 1986 (no. 2) Education Acts.

The way in which parental choice is to be enhanced is largely by restricting the power of LEAs to manage (or circumvent) the operation of choice. Parents have in many areas been able to express a preference for particular county or voluntary schools, and the 1980 Act required LEAs to comply with that preference unless the school in question regulated its admissions 'by reference to ability or aptitude', or was a voluntary school with an admissions policy incompatible with the parental preference, or unless the LEA took the view that 'compliance with the preference would prejudice the provision of efficient education or the efficient use of resources' (1980 Education Act, s. 6(3)). These were important caveats. (Some research into how LEAs responded to them is discussed in chapter 3.) In particular the third proviso, about efficient use of resources, allowed LEAs if they so wished to regulate the intake to all their schools, whatever their relative popularity with parents.

The whole question of admissions, as dealt with in legislation during the 1980s, has to be seen in the light of falling rolls during that decade. Just as, following the 1944 Education Act, the 'wishes of parents' were never studied in isolation from the 'roofs over heads' preoccupations of the expanding education system following the Second World War, so in the 1980s concern about pupil population decline has accompanied all considerations of parental choice. Pupil numbers peaked around 1977 but the crude birth rate had been falling since 1965. Throughout the 1980s the numbers of school-age children were in steep decline. Early in the decade local authorities were called on by government to make appropriate reductions in the number of available school places. Some authorities put in hand a programme of school closures; others decided to spread out the pupil intake so that all schools remained viable institutions with an adequate, if diminished, flow of pupils. All of these arrangements could be put forward as 'efficient use of resources', justifying possible non-compliance with parental preference for particular schools.

However the Education Reform Act gives a new priority to parental preference. The main effect of its admissions sections is to inhibit the arbitrary imposition of top admission limits on individual schools. School admission limits must be based on an analysis of teaching places in the school, that is, the physical room which exists for pupils, rather than on, for example, the present pupil–teacher ratio. Schools must admit pupils up to a 'standard number' which represents the limits of their physical capacity.[23] This is not to say that open enrolment will prevail, despite much loose use of this term. Schools are not required to *expand* to meet demand. If the local authority or (in the case of a voluntary school) the governors want to significantly enlarge the premises of the school to accommodate more pupils, they must publish proposals to do so (under sections 12 or 13 of the 1980 Act). But schools cannot be deemed 'oversubscribed' because of any pupil allocation decision by the LEA. If parents want their child to attend a particular school (and therefore *not* to attend some other school in the authority to which he or she might otherwise have been directed), their wish must be complied with up to the limits of the school's physical capacity.

The idea implicit in this part of the 1988 Act seems to be the promotion of individual freedom of the citizen parent to make a choice of school for the child, rather than the state (as represented by the local education authority). We shall see later that this idea may conflict with other ideas embodied in other parts of the Act.

Objections to the 1988 Act's enhancement of parental choice have followed three main themes. The first is the 'planning' objection which, as we have seen, has been voiced by Ranson (1990) among others. It may be both inefficient and unfair to future generations of children to allow parental choice to govern the distribution of children between schools, at a time of falling rolls. The resultant closure of temporarily unpopular schools may mean that in future the geographical spread of available school places will be inequitable.[24] However it should be noted that the draft circular giving guidance on the implementation of the Act points out that if authorities remove accommodation when demand for places is low, they may have to replace it later if demand revives (DES, 1988, para. 29).

A second theme of objection is the assertion that all individual freedoms are not mutually compatible. During the consultative period of the Bill (see note 22), the Association of County Councils (ACC) endorsed the importance of paying the closest possible attention to the wishes of parents, but saw a practical problem when 'a marginal increase in meeting the preferences of some has to be set against a general reduction in the preferences of others'. Their claim was that there were educational (not just geographical) grounds for spreading reduced admission numbers evenly. 'If numbers at one or two schools are allowed to run down too greatly while the others remain full to capacity, the quality of education in the undersubscribed schools will suffer and they will be more costly to maintain than if all had a reasonable share of the numbers' (ACC, *Take Care Mr Baker!* [hereafter TCMB], p. 177). This is obviously a variant of the 'efficiency' argument, but one which stresses the possible effect on a school of surviving with reduced numbers, rather than closing down because of a totally unviable intake.

A third theme of opposition to the Bill's proposals for admissions was that a change in admission limits would encourage schools to 'set themselves in the market-place, losing sight of their true purpose and directing the energies of their staff into areas which have little to do with the education of children . . . the competitive ethos will permeate a school's organisation at the cost of education philosophy' (Headmaster of Hove Park School, East Sussex, TCMB, p. 189). Some would contend, however, that maintained schools are already in the market-place. They compete with the co-existing independent schools, and with each other in that the number of available children is finite, whatever arrangements by the LEA may influence their allocation. Some training for school management now embraces the need to market the school.[25]

A NATIONAL CURRICULUM

The introduction of a national curriculum, it has been suggested, represents 'the largest single change in the provision of education in schools since the implementation of the 1944 Education Act' (ACC, TCMB, p. 37). Certainly the national curriculum is central to the 1988 Education Reform Act, and provoked a storm in the educational world, eliciting more responses to the consultative document at the bill stage than any other provision. But what is its relevance for parental choice?

The Act requires every maintained school (with the exception of special schools) to teach a national curriculum comprising core and foundation subjects,[26] in respect of which certain attainment targets, programmes of study and assessment arrangements will prevail. Broadly the intention (set out in the consultative document) was that children should be entitled to the same opportunities wherever they went to school, and that standards of attainment should be raised throughout England and Wales. All pupils, 'regardless of sex, ethnic origin and geographical location', should have access to broadly the same good and relevant curriculum' (DES, 1987a, p. 4).

If uniformly implemented, a national curriculum will reduce parental choice of schools to non-curricular aspects. If unevenly implemented, however, the Act gives parents the right to complain specifically about professional curricular decisions which were formerly the province of the school. These complaints would be made to the LEA or the appropriate governing body, and not directly to the secretary of state. The power of the governing body (including parent governors) to influence each school's curriculum in the light of local needs (a power provided in the 1986 (No. 2) Act) may seem to be largely negated by the introduction of a national curriculum, but it should be noted that governors of grant-maintained schools (discussed below), schools which are also subject to national curriculum requirements, are explicitly required to take account of local representations when considering the content of the secular curriculum (Education Reform Act 1988, s. 58(5)(i)). This would seem to imply that the similar clauses of the 1986 Act (ss 18(3) and (6)) still apply to county and voluntary schools.

The content of the curriculum is the aspect which has aroused the greatest controversy, but for our purposes it is the overall *concept* of a national curriculum which is most relevant. It embodies the idea of equal education discussed earlier in this chapter, and specifies what education is 'needed' during the compulsory school years. Equality, as we saw earlier, is a principle which has been more often invoked in opposition to parental choice than in support of it, and in effect the 'equality' offered by a national curriculum will reduce parental choice by reducing some aspects of the diversity of schools. What the Act assumes, however, is that parents will not *want* to choose a school which does not offer the national curriculum. Their main aim will be to ensure that the school does effectively deliver this curriculum, and that each pupil has access to it 'regardless of' the child's sex or ethnic origin. In other words, there is deemed to be a consensus about the 'needed' aspects of education, a consensus which is unaffected by a child's particular characteristics.[27] The national curriculum both assumes and would arguably promote social cohesion, another principle which, as we have seen, to some extent belies choice.

Where choice re-enters the debate, however, is in how well individual schools deliver the curriculum. The 1988 Act adds to the information which schools were already required to provide to parents by the 1980 Education Act. New information will cover the 'educational achievements of pupils at the school (including the results of any assessments of those pupils . . . for the purpose of ascertaining those achievements' (1988 Act, s. 22(2)(c)). This suggests a model of parental choice which relies on prior information, then leaves the conduct of the school to the professionals. However the parent will also have access to regular information about their own child's attainments (tested against national standards) within the school he or she attends, which may provide some leverage on the school itself.

Once again, it is of interest to see what ideas were invoked during the consultative phase, either in support of or in opposition to the proposals of a national curriculum. Very few interested parties opposed the concept, but much energy was spent in critical commentary on the proposed content of the curriculum, in particular its subject-based rather than child-centred approach. The legislation as enacted has taken account of complaints about the marginal status accorded to religious education in the consultation document, and this now stands with the core subjects at the heart of the curriculum. The subject-oriented basis of the curriculum remained unaltered, however, and continued to be the subject of controversy as various subject working groups did their work.[28]

Another across-the-board criticism was of the lack of resources to implement the new curriculum. The National Association of Headteachers (NAHT), among others, said that parents might assert their rights by complaining, but there was no resource framework to enable the legislative curriculum to be delivered (NAHT, TCMB, pp. 24–5).

One of the criticisms most relevant to parental choice was the assertion that in aiming for equal entitlement to a national curriculum the Act overlooks pluralism in society. 'References to parents in the [consultative] document imply that they share broadly similar feelings of dissatisfaction with schools'. It fails to 'grasp the nettle of conflicting parental views and expectations'. Rather than operating 'regardless' of ethnic origins, for example, curricular delivery should be 'mindful' of such differences and the needs they imply (Association of LEA Advisory Officers for Multicultural Education, TCMB, p. 46). This argument harks back to Coons and Sugarman's theme that there is no consensus in society and individual parents know best their own child's need.

As an embodiment of developing education policy during the 1980s to strengthen the position of parents, the Reform Act's national curriculum proposals were perhaps most relevantly criticized by the National Confederation of Parent-Teacher Associations (NCPTA), which claimed the legislation to impose a national curriculum seemed 'contrary to the spirit of the 1986 Education Act which has . . . given to school governors the responsibility to consider the LEA policy for the secular curriculum and to decide whether it should be modified for their particular school' (NCPTA, TCMB, p. 33). However, as we saw earlier, this responsibility does not seem to have been removed, although its scope has surely been restricted.

GRANT-MAINTAINED SCHOOLS

The 1988 Education Reform Act enabled the transfer of maintained schools to a new kind of status, one in which the secretary of state would directly make the necessary payments in respect of their expenses. In other words, such schools would be maintained by direct grants from central government, rather than via local education authorities.[29] In introducing the possibility of this new status for schools, the consultative document suggested that 'the greater diversity of provision . . . should enhance the prospect of improving standards in schools' (DES, 1987, para. 2).

As with any change in the structure of educational provision, at least as much attention has focused on the process of the change itself as on the future life of the new institutions. During the progress of the Education Reform Bill through Parliament, and following its enactment, reference has continually been made to 'opting out' (of local education authority control) rather than to the more positive activity of 'becoming a grant-maintained school'. Many interested parties have concluded that the first purpose of this part of the Reform Act is, for good or ill, to weaken the hold of the LEA on the local education system (TCMB: Society of Education Officers, p. 124; Liverpool City Council, p. 119; London Borough of Barnet, p. 120; Social Democratic Party, p. 116). The Act itself necessarily devotes much space to the process of transfer from local-authority-maintained to grant-maintained status. What is the role of parents, both in the transfer procedure and the subsequent conduct of the schools?

There are three prerequisites for grant-maintained status. First, the school must be eligible for the status. In the terms of the Act, all maintained secondary schools (whether county or voluntary) and all primary schools with at least 300 pupils on roll, are eligible.[30] Subsequently, the Act makes clear, even the smaller primary schools may be made eligible by an order from the secretary of state. Secondly, schools seeking grant-maintained status must publish proposals to this end, in an agreed form. Thirdly, those proposals must receive the approval of the secretary of state.

Parents of pupils currently at the school are the gatekeepers to the whole process, in that they must all be invited to participate in a postal ballot before proposals to apply to grant-maintained status can be published. Only if at least 50 per cent of eligible parents take part in the ballot, and a majority of these are in favour of the change,[31] can the proposals go forward. Here, then, is an important new moment of choice for some parents. If the idea of transfer has emanated from the governing body (with or without the support of the headteacher), but parents vote against it in the ballot, the proposals cannot proceed further (although the process may be reactivated after twelve months). Alternatively, it may be a group of parents (at least twenty per cent of the parent body) who have initiated the idea. Once again, the view of balloted parents will govern its progress to the published proposals stage, or its abandonment.[32]

The status of being the parent of a pupil registered at a school has assumed a new significance through these sections of the Reform Act. Hitherto, although only parents of registered pupils were entitled to vote for parent governors, no special steps had to be taken to ensure that all eligible parents had the opportunity to vote. Because of the possible balloting of parents about grant-maintained status, however, governors are now required to maintain a list of all parents whose child is a pupil at the school (s. 60(7)). This list is not confined to parents having custody of the child, and should include parents living at separate addresses. The ballot itself is required to be conducted by secret postal vote.

If parents have a key role in the process of seeking grant-maintained status, what will be their role in the conduct of a school which acquires that status? The Reform Act lays great stress on the constitution and responsibilities of the governing bodies of grant-maintained schools. These responsibilities include having full control of the school's budget (not by 'delegation' from the LEA), and becoming the employer of the school's staff – governing bodies will not be required to involve the LEA in appointments and dismissals. Parents of pupils currently at the school will have a sizeable representation on the governing body, but they will not outnumber other governors. 'First' governors (or, in the case of voluntary schools, 'foundation' governors) will be the largest group on the governing body. At least two of these may be parents of pupils at the school, but most will be 'persons appearing to be members of the local community committed to the good government and continuing viability of the school', and in the case of former county (rather than voluntary) schools, will include persons 'appearing to be members of the local business community'. In the (minimally envisaged) governing body of seventeen, at least nine would be first or foundation governors, the remainder being elected parent governors (five), elected teacher governors (a maximum of two) and the headteacher. If numbers are the criterion, it seems that the voice of parents will be slightly less important in the governing body of grant-maintained schools than in other maintained schools.[33]

So far as parental choice of school is concerned, grant-maintained schools will indeed bring further diversity to the system of maintained education, and on that score will extend choice. Grant-maintained schools will differ from other schools in their relationships with local and central government, and perhaps in their motivation to make a success of handling their own affairs, including their motivation to raise supplementary funds by a variety of means.[34] In other ways, however, at least initially, schools will not be transformed by becoming grant-maintained. Admission policy must be similar to when the school had county status. For voluntary schools which become grant-maintained, the articles of government must comply with the original trust deed.[35]

Whatever the origins of the school, any changes in the character or premises of a grant-maintained school would have to be the subject of published proposals, objections to which could be submitted to the secretary of state, whose approval the proposals would require. The Reform Act defines the 'character' of a school somewhat broadly as concerning the 'provision of education at the school' and 'the arrangements for admission of pupils to the school' (s. 104(c)). More specifically, the Act states that

> references to a change in the character of a school include, in particular, changes in character resulting from education beginning or ceasing to be provided for pupils above or below a particular age, for boys as well as girls or for girls as well as boys, or from the making or alteration of arrangements for the admission of pupils by reference to ability or aptitude.
>
> (1988 Education Reform Act, s. 104(d))

Criticisms of the introduction of grant-maintained schools at the consultative stage were numerous. They tended not unnaturally to focus on the loss of control by the LEA if schools 'opted out'. Some contributors to the debate welcomed the schools as an increase of consumer choice (Conservative Family campaign, TCMB, p. 132), but most emphasized the unsuitability of parents to be the arbiters of educational decisions involving institutional change. We saw earlier in this chapter that the incapacity of parents is one aspect of parental choice which often features in educational debate if not in face to face discussion with parents. However it was the transience of parents' involvement with a school which was chiefly stressed by critics of the Bill, and the inequity of allowing one cohort of parents to influence a decision which would affect staff, pupils and other parents for years to come (TCMB: Professional Association of Teachers, p. 112; National Association of Governors and Managers, p. 129; Special Educational Needs, National Advisory Council, p. 133). A number of commentators took the line that choice would be *reduced* by the introduction of grant-maintained schools (TCMB: SEO, p. 125; ACC p. 123). Their thought appeared to be that the presence of a grant-maintained school in an area deprived parents by giving them one less locally maintained school to choose from.

We have already noted that equality is an important theme of consideration where parental choice is concerned. Critics of the creation of grant-maintained schools laid emphasis on the effect such schools might have on equality of education opportunity. The schools would be seen to be different in their source of funding and their management style, and might attract particular types of families. This, they claimed, would be divisive. They also envisaged the possibility that certain religious or ethnic groups, interested in having exclusive schools funded by the state, might seek to 'opt in' to grant-maintained status. The Centre for Policy Studies (TCMB, p. 105) favoured this idea, but others considered it would 'undermine principles of social cohesiveness in a pluralist society' (National Union of Teachers, TCMB, p. 131). Another group, the Campaign for the Advancement of State Education (CASE) went further, suggesting that the plan for grant-maintained schools, along with the Reform Bill's proposals for 'open enrolment' would lead to 'racial tension and ultimately apartheid' (CASE, TCMB, p. 135).

A prominent theme of objections to the new type of school was that such a proposal should not have been introduced alongside other wide-ranging proposals for change in education. Several parts of the Bill, concerned with admission policies, the national curriculum and local financial management, had the overall aim of raising standards in schools. These should have been allowed to work through into practice before introducing any new institution such as the grant-maintained school which might, in the event, be an unnecessary further attempt to raise standards (College of Preceptors, TCMB, p. 131). In any case, their advent should have been delayed until the admission proposals had time to work through and 'weed out' unpopular schools. The possibility of grant-maintained status was likely to slow down the process of schools' rationalization (Audit Commission, TCMB, p. 108).

However, as we know, the Education Reform Act went through in its blockbuster form, and grant-maintained schools were not the only new institutional form which it introduced.

CITY COLLEGES

Unlike the lengthy portion of the Reform Act devoted to grant-maintained schools (ss 52–104), both city technology colleges and city colleges for the technology of the arts are introduced within the compass of a single section (s. 105), the first three subsections of which are reproduced below.

(1) The Secretary of State may enter into an agreement with any person under which –

(a) that person undertakes to establish and maintain, and to carry on or provide for the carrying on of either –

(i) an independent school to be known as a city technology college; or

(ii) an independent school to be known as a city college for the technology of the arts;

and having (in each case) such characteristics as are specified in the agreement and in subsection (2) below; and

(b) the Secretary of State agrees to make payments to that person in consideration of those undertakings.

(2) The characteristics mentioned above are that the school –

(a) is situated in an urban area;

(b) provides education for pupils of different abilities who have attained the age of eleven years but not the age of nineteen years and who are wholly or mainly drawn from the area in which the school is situated; and

(c) has a broad curriculum with an emphasis –

(i) in the case of a school to be known as a city technology college, on science and technology; or

(ii) in the case of a school to be known as a city college for the technology of the arts, on technology in its application to the performing and creative arts.

(3) An agreement under this section shall make any payments by the Secretary of State dependent on the fulfilment of –

(a) conditions and requirements imposed for the purpose of securing that no charge is made in respect of admission to the school or, subject to such exceptions as may be specified in the agreement, in respect of education provided at the school; and

(b) such other conditions and requirements with respect to the school as are specified in the agreement.

(1988 Education Reform Act, s. 105)

In essence, what the Act introduces is a new type of secondary school, funding for which comes both from private sources and from central government. These city colleges, called 'independent' in the Act, will be distinguished from other independent schools both by their sources of funding and by the requirement that no fees are charged to pupils, who should be 'of different abilities' and drawn from the urban locality in which the school is situated.

As independent schools the city colleges will not be required to follow the national curriculum. Indeed, one purpose of their creation is that their curriculum shall display a particular emphasis (see s. 105(c) above).

Like the grant-maintained schools, the city colleges enlarge the range of parental choice.[36] They are hybrid institutions, neither maintained nor fully independent. Their style and development will depend considerably on the terms of the agreement entered into with the secretary of state. Larger sums of public money than envisaged at the outset have already been devoted to their establishment (Maclure, 1988, p. 120). For the time being the colleges stand very much alone, neither fellows to the independent fee-paying schools nor to the maintained county and voluntary schools.[37]

The Act's provision for these new colleges appears to indicate central government's wish to blur the distinction between privately funded and publicly funded education, at the same time extending the range of institutions where education is free to the user (a concept further discussed in chapter 2). Early publicity material about the colleges gave the impression that to succeed in gaining a place for their child, parents would need to convince the college authorities that they both understood the particular curricular emphasis of the college and were prepared to give it their support.

The assumed demand for these colleges places reliance on the belief expounded by Coons and Sugarman (1978) that families know their child, can assess his or her educational needs, and will benefit from the availability of a range of educational institutions which provide distinctive types of education.

Conclusion

The 1988 Act has indeed re-formed education. For the foreseeable future the main parties to education – central government, local government, headteachers and staff, school governors, parents and their children – find themselves in a new relationship. Central government is taking a closer and more focused interest in schooling, through the national curriculum. Local government enters an experimental phase, in which it will entrust schools with greater independence (through LMS), while standing by them in a more advisory capacity, like a parent with an adolescent child. Heads, teachers and governors are linked together in much closer partnership regarding the affairs of the school. Some may conclude they no longer need their link with the LEA, and may opt out from its control.[38]

Parents of school pupils, with their children, are affected by all these changes and have a role to play in many of them. Most of all, through new arrangements for admissions to schools, they can vote with their feet about the future pattern of schooling. School funding will be largely based on pupil numbers, and parents hold the key which opens the flow of resources to particular schools.

Arguments about parents' right and capacity to choose their children's schools will continue, but the *fact* of parental choice as a mainstream policy is with us as we enter the 1990s. In chapters 5 and 6 we look at some of the effects of a policy for parental choice on LEAs, schools and families, and consider whether choice is likely to be an important agent for change in education. Meanwhile, in chapter 2 we examine present diversity in education and the scope for choice which exists, before reviewing in chapters 3 and 4 what research has already revealed about the exercise of parental choice of school.

Chapter 2

The scope of choice

The great majority of school-age children attend the maintained primary and secondary schools which are local to their home. Were their parents conscious of making a choice, when entering into this arrangement? Were they aware of the full range of educational forms which are on offer? We cannot be sure. Some of the research which has been carried out into how parents made school choices before the 1988 Education Reform Act will be discussed in chapters 3 and 4. At the time of writing, no formal research study has been completed of how parents respond to their new opportunities for choice. Now that parents are being encouraged to see the family as the prime decision-maker in where a child goes to school, it may be that more families will make the deliberate and detailed choices about their children's education which a small proportion of families have made in the past. Whether they will do so in the full knowledge of all the forms of education which are available seems doubtful. Not many consumer choices are made with perfect knowledge of the market concerned, but some attempt should be made to find out what scope exists.

Teachers know more than most people about the diversity within our education system, but few have encountered all its variety. This chapter sets out to fill a gap in knowledge by systematically discussing the range of schooling in England. It offers an overview of the many forms of schooling about which parents might want to express a preference, then discusses some of the ways in which parents are helped or hindered from making choices.

Local diversity is a feature of education in England.[1] This diversity is a product of local history, and of party political pressures and other interest group pressures at both a local and national level. County, voluntary and independent schools exist side by side. Most schools handle only a narrow age-range of pupils, but some offer education on an all-through basis. Most schools are co-educational, but some accept only boys or girls. Some schools are selective by ability, many are not. Most pupils live at home and go to school on a daily basis but some schools, in both the public and the private sectors, are residential.

The main educational alternatives are:

- public or private
- 'free' or fee-paying
- selective or non-selective (by various criteria)
- strongly or nominally religious
- residential or non-residential
- single sex or co-educational
- all-through or age-related
- institutional or home-based

These are almost all tendentious choices, and most people will have a view about whether such choices should or should not be available. These educational and ideological positions will only be referred to in passing here. The main purpose is simply to set the scene in which parental choice is exercised.

Public or private schooling

Most democracies in the Western world have both private schools and state schools, and signatories to the European Convention on Human Rights may not limit education to that provided by the state.

In England in 1987, the year preceding the Education Reform Act and its introduction of grant-maintained schools, nearly seven million pupils received their education in 23,653 schools maintained by local education authorities with public money derived from central and local taxes. Alongside the massive 'state' system, in 1987 half a million pupils were educated in 2,276 private schools, some of which were run as businesses, and others as educational trusts, with charitable status.

It has become the tradition in much writing about maintained education to ignore the private schools, except perhaps to allege that they 'cream' the best pupils from the public sector (Rutter *et al.*, 1979; Bush and Kogan, 1982; Gray *et al.*, 1983; Hall, Mackay and Morgan, 1986). A separate literature examines the private sector from a more positive point of view (see for example, Honey, 1977; Rae, 1981; Leinster-Mackay, 1984; Fox, 1985; Walford, 1986). However, there are a number of reasons why a book on parental choice should take an even-handed look at both forms of education. Although the private sector is small compared with the maintained sector, it provides, in some parts of the country, a reference point for parents who are trying to evaluate the strengths of particular maintained schools, and it represents an aspect of choice which is carefully considered by some parents. More families make some use of private education than would appear from the annual head-counting of pupils which features in DES statistics. It is not always the same heads which are counted, since families may move their children between public and private education several times during their school years. From a policy point of view the histories of the two sectors of education have always been intertwined, and considerable use is still made of private schools by public authorities for pupils who cannot be catered for in the maintained sector (Johnson, 1987).

The state sector of education now has three strands – county, voluntary and grant-maintained schools. County schools are fully provided and maintained by local education authorities. Voluntary schools have been provided by an educational trust, usually a religious society; their maintenance may be a shared responsibility.[2] Grant-maintained schools, outside local authority control and funded directly by central government, are a new development, as we saw in Chapter 1. It is too soon to say whether grant-maintained schools will in due course become a homogeneous group within the maintained sector, exhibiting certain characteristic features.

While the main unit of organization in the public education sector is still the local education authority,[3] most private schools are free-standing individual institutions, some of them loosely affiliated by associations of varying rigour and esteem,[4] but others quite autonomous in their action. A few private schools, such as those belonging to the Girls' Public Day Schools Trust, operate as consortia.

All schools, both public and private, are approved by H.M. Inspectorate (HMI), make annual statistical returns to the Department of Education and Science (DES), and are subject to inspection by HMI. Legal requirements for compulsory education between the ages of 5 and 16 may be met by attendance either at a maintained or a private school. In 1987 the balance of usage (not necessarily the balance of *preference*) between public and private education in England and Wales was 93 per cent public, 7 per cent private.

'Free' or fee-paying education

No form of education is without cost. The notion of 'free' education refers to schooling funded from public money, which is free to the user at the point of access. The 1944 Education Act (s. 61(1)) requires that no fees be charged for admission to schools maintained by local education authorities. Even before the 1944 Education Act, elementary state education for children aged 5 to 14 years had been non-fee paying, but nominal means-tested fees were payable for selective secondary education in some local authority areas, until the 1944 Act.

Although no county or voluntary school has ever contravened the 1944 Act by charging a straight attendance fee, some controversies have arisen from time to time about the charging of fees for individual music tuition, cookery costs and other curriculum-related outlay. In voluntary aided schools, where fifteen per cent of certain capital costs has to be met by the governors on behalf of the Foundation,[5] parents are invariably asked to make regular voluntary contributions to the schools. Frequently they are asked to 'covenant' these payments. Some parents have felt under undue pressure to make these 'voluntary' payments, and in 1987 a complaint by parents of pupils at several Jewish voluntary aided schools was brought to the attention of the secretary of state, with the claim that the 'free education' principle of the 1944 Education Act was being contravened. A subsequent enquiry by the secretary of state and the LEA concerned concluded that improper pressure may well have been put upon parents, and the governors were required to change the procedure under which they solicited genuinely voluntary contributions.[6]

Some grey areas of dubious practice in maintained schools have now been clarified by the 1988 Education Reform Act, which permits the charging of fees for individual tuition in playing a musical instrument and for the provision of board and lodging for the pupil while on a residential trip arranged on behalf of the governing body or the local education authority. Charges may also be made in respect of educational activities including residential trips which in the terms of the Act take place outside school hours.[7] However, no charge may be made for registered pupils' education (other than individual music tuition) during school hours, and this applies equally to voluntary, county and grant-maintained schools.

City colleges, as we saw in chapter 1, are hybrid institutions: neither fully independent nor fully publicly maintained. The colleges may not charge fees for admission or education, but according to the terms of the agreement entered into between the secretary of state and the founders of the college, they may receive public money for capital or current expenditure.

The broad principle of the 1944 Act still stands with respect to 'free' public education. It is open to every citizen to choose this type of education for his or her child.

One of the distinguishing features of private, as opposed to state, schools is that fees are charged to parents (the few exceptions to this general rule will be discussed later). In 1987, the average fee per term for a place in a preparatory school (ages 4 to 13 approximately) was £710; for a girl's senior day school £732; and a boy's senior day school £784. These figures are based on statistics from schools affiliated with the Independent Schools Information Service (ISIS), which were supplied to ISIS in January 1988. It could be said that 'choice' of a private school is limited to those who can afford these fees for their children's education. The great majority of places in private education are indeed paid for in full by parents. However, numerous arrangements exist whereby a child's fees may be met from a scholarship fund, or paid by a local authority or the DES, usually in cases of special educational need or special talent (Johnson, 1987). Another source of financial support is the Assisted Places scheme, laid down by the 1980 Education Act, which enables certain independent schools to offer some free or assisted places to children from low income families, the remitted fees being made up from public money. In 1987 the private school fees of almost 10,000 pupils were paid in full by the DES under this scheme, and a further 14,500 had part of their fees met by the scheme (figures supplied by the Assisted Places Unit, DES). The operation of the Assisted Places scheme and other sources of public money for independent school fees are more fully discussed in a later section of this chapter.

Many fee-paying schools were originally endowed by charitable trusts for the education of poor scholars. Some of the well-known private boarding schools for boys, often referred to as public schools, are in this category. Most of these schools now educate only the sons of families who can meet their substantial fees, but long-standing endowments continue to supplement the resources of these schools. However a few such schools, notably Christ's Hospital, continue to admit only children from low-income families. Fees are subsidized, and numerous free places are provided from endowments. Additionally, individual children may be nominated for a place by benefactors of the school whose donations supplement existing endowments.

Other schools which in some cases have dispensed with fee-charging are the Rudolph Steiner or Waldorf schools. Some (but not all) of these schools have attempted to rely on voluntary contributions from parents. The informality of this arrangement has however caused some difficulty when a local education authority has been prepared to sponsor a child at such a school, which they deem suitable to meet his or her special educational needs. When the local authority is paying, a clear fee has to be stipulated. This and other difficulties have discouraged the schools from continuing to operate on a voluntary payments basis (Johnson, 1987).

Certain other 'free' schools exist which rely on parental contributions rather than fees, but these are usually part-time or Saturday schools, attended as a supplement to regular schooling in another maintained or private school. Many of these schools are organized by and for particular nationals or ethnic groups, such as Poles, Chinese, West Indian or Asian children. These arrangements cannot be described as 'alternative' schooling, as attendance at such a school does not satisfy the statutory requirement for compulsory education. Genuinely 'alternative' forms of schooling, such as by correspondence or approved home tuition, are discussed in a later section of this chapter.

Selective or non-selective education

Many different criteria may be applied to the selection of children for particular schools. Not all are overt. Some of the less openly expressed – or perhaps more taken for granted – criteria will be discussed later. But in educational parlance, 'selective' schooling is usually a shorthand term for a principle of selection based on academic ability. The exercise, or abandonment, of this principle has done more to separate public from private education than any other factor.[8]

In the maintained sector access to primary education is not subject to selection by academic ability. Trends of parental choice for particular schools (whether county or voluntary) may tend to skew the range of academic ability of pupils accepted on to roll, but this is not the principle of their acceptance. At the secondary stage, however, for some twenty years following the 1944 Act, the 11 plus examination was used in most LEAs to allocate pupils to grammar schools, secondary modern schools and a few technical schools, on the basis of differing ability. In the 1980s, some LEAs still retain their academically selective grammar schools, but most secondary schools are comprehensive in their organization. The principle of comprehensivization has spread throughout the maintained education system since the mid-1960s. Some LEAs, such as Hertfordshire, prefer the designation 'all-ability' schools to that of 'comprehensive'. Whatever the name, the principle is that a child's ability is not a criterion for allocation to a school. Comprehensive schools aim to provide the education appropriate for children across the full range of ability. Prior to the 1988 Reform Act, places at particular schools were allocated by the LEA on a variety of administrative or educational grounds: local residence, sibling attendance, linking of primary schools with particular secondary schools and/or (to a greater or lesser extent) the expression of parental choice. Since the 1988 Act, as we have seen, parental choice has to be given higher priority.

At voluntary secondary schools which control their own admissions, a comprehensive intake is also the usually expressed policy. Local opinion sometimes doubts the implementation of this policy, but it is probably the case that, as with popular primary schools, parental preferences for particular voluntary secondary schools tend to skew the academic intake, more than the possible exercise of academic selection by the governors or head.

City colleges, which in the terms of the Education Reform Act 1988 (s. 105) may be either city technology colleges or city colleges for the technology of the arts, are not intended to be selective by particular forms of ability, whether 'technical' or otherwise. The colleges are required to be 'situated in an urban area' and to provide 'education for pupils of different abilities who have attained the age of eleven years but not the age of nineteen years and who are wholly or mainly drawn from the area in which the school is situated' (s. 105(2)(a) and (b)). Motivation of parents and child to pursue the particular form of education these colleges offer is, it appears, intended to be the chief criterion for allocation of a place.

In private education, some form of appraisal precedes all admissions, even at the age of five years. Admissions to private schools are of individuals, not of age cohorts. LEAs *must* offer a school place to any child of school age living in the authority. Private schools are under no such obligation. Independent schools in England educate only 500,000 children, compared with some 7 million in maintained schools. In any given area, relatively few private school places are available.[9] Demand for these places may vary sharply from school to school, but all admissions imply a contract between school and parent, so some kind of mutual appraisal takes place.

The general impression prevails that private education is highly selective on an academic basis. Whilst this is not true of all private schools, few of them would claim to be all-ability or comprehensive in their intake. Certainly the well established direct grant schools declined to embrace the comprehensive principle when invited to do so following the second report of the Public Schools Commission in 1970. The majority of them gave up their government funding at least partly in order to retain their 'grammar school' selective admission policies. Direct grant status was phased out in 1975.[10]

Ex-direct grant schools, many other highly regarded independent secondary schools and also their junior departments, continue to hold entrance examinations which drastically sift applications. A much reduced body of applicants then proceeds through further forms of selection, usually by interview. Not all the criteria of selection are academic, although the entrance examination has already made the first cull on this basis. At one such school where 66 places were available, as many as 200 boys who had come through the entrance exam would be interviewed. The headteacher considered that 'somewhere at the bottom of the acceptable exam mark range he might find "a nugget of gold", in the shape of a boy with particular musical artistic or sporting gifts, or certain qualities of temperament'. Candidates' parents were also interviewed, at this and other independent schools. For the head of one preparatory school, the attitude of the parents was paramount in his yearly selection of an intake of twenty-five boys. 'Basically, if I like the parent, I will have the child. I have got to work with those parents for nine years. If I dislike the parents, even if the boy is bright I wouldn't have him' (Johnson, 1987, p. 63).

Many would-be entrants to these independent schools have been previously educated in the maintained sector. The most usual stages at which this kind of cross-sector transfer is sought are ages 7/8 (when, within the maintained sector the movement from infant to junior, or first to middle, school takes place), or age 10/11, the primary to secondary transfer stage. Many independent schools now have a major intake procedure, with entrance exams and an interview programme, at age 11.

Pupils already attending independent schools sit Common Entrance at age 13, following which they transfer to the independent senior school which offers them a place. Common Entrance is also an academically selective procedure, with an (unpublished) pecking-order of schools which accept applicants at different academic levels. But in many independent day schools, the 11 year-old intake is more important for the school's roll than the 13 year-old intake.

Strongly religious or nominally religious education

The opportunity for an entirely secular form of schooling does not exist in British public education, at the time of writing.[11] This situation may be contrasted with the secular position of public education in the USA, where the teaching of religion and religious practices are unlawful in public schools, and schools of religious orientation may not benefit from public funds.[12] Nor is a fully secular education to be found in the private sector in Britain. However in both sectors some schools have a much clearer religious orientation than others, and it is this variation which will chiefly be discussed here.

COUNTY SCHOOLS

The 1944 Education Act required all county schools to provide religious education according to an agreed syllabus, and laid down that 'the school day in every county school and in every voluntary school shall begin with collective worship on the part of all pupils in attendance' (1944 Act, s. 25). This was an entirely new statutory requirement. By the terms of the 1944 Act religion is therefore required to be both taught and practised, in a non-denominational form, in all county schools in the United Kingdom. Parents may, if they wish, withdraw their children from these activities, but the activities continue. In the 1970s and 1980s it was frequently pointed out (Souper and Kay, 1983) that school assemblies had ceased to be whole-school affairs, and in many cases were no longer in any real sense describable as acts of collective worship. Nevertheless the 1988 Education Reform Act has reaffirmed the requirement for all pupils at maintained schools on each school day to take part in an act of collective worship, though arrangements may now be made for 'a single act of worship for all pupils or for separate acts of worship for pupils in different age groups or in different school groups' (Education Reform Act 1988, s. 6(2)). And it has added a stipulation which the 1944 Act omitted, namely that the collective worship in county schools[13] shall be 'wholly or mainly of a broadly Christian character' (s. 7(1)).

As for the place of religious education as a curricular subject, we saw in the previous chapter that, after much debate during the passage of the Education Reform Bill, religious education has become a core element of the national curriculum to be provided for all registered pupils.[14] Where an agreed syllabus is followed, this 'shall reflect the fact that the religious traditions in Great Britain are in the main Christian whilst taking account of the teaching and practices of the other principal religions represented in Great Britain' (Education Reform Act 1988, s. 8(3)).

VOLUNTARY SCHOOLS

The non-secular orientation of county schools has been re-emphasised by the Education Reform Act. Nevertheless, it is the voluntary schools which make up the most overtly 'religious' strand of our public education. Two religious societies (one Anglican, one Nonconformist),[15] soon followed by a Catholic group,[16] were the first providers of elementary education in England and Wales, before the 1870 Education Act created Board schools to fill the gaps in the religious societies' provision. From 1902 these schools of religious foundation were known as 'non-provided' schools, but were partly maintained by local taxes.[17] In 1944 the religious schools, henceforward referred to as voluntary schools, were brought fully into the public sector of education. Most of these schools were for the primary age group, but some 'special agreement' voluntary schools, set up in the 1930s, were organized as secondary modern schools. All other voluntary schools, by the terms of the 1944 Act, had to choose either 'aided' or 'controlled' status. Controlled schools were those which agreed to fall in fully with the practices of the county schools, teaching religious education according to an agreed syllabus, accepting full funding from the local authority and having all their staff appointed or dismissed by the LEA, with the sole exception of 'reserved teachers' recruited by the school's governors specifically to provide the relevant denominational form of religious teaching for those families requesting this (1944 Education Act, s. 27).

Voluntary aided schools, however, had and have a different status. Their governing body, which includes a substantial number of governors appointed by the religious bodies with an interest in the school[18] appoints and dismisses all teaching staff,[19] and has responsibility for funding 15 per cent of certain capital expenditure and for external repairs to the school building. The governors of special agreement schools have similar responsibilities. The admission of pupils to voluntary aided and special agreement schools is also a matter of policy for the governors, and this is one of the important features of these schools so far as parental choice is concerned.

In 1987, 35 per cent of all primary schools and 20 per cent of all secondary schools in England were of voluntary status, 39 per cent of all full-time primary school pupils and 22 per cent of all secondary school pupils attended these schools. Table 2.1 shows the number and types of voluntary school which existed in the maintained sector of education in England, in 1987.

Table 2.1 Numbers and types of voluntary schools in England, 1987

		Controlled	Aided	Special Agreement	Total
Church of England	primary	2859	1937	1	4797
	secondary	95	120	18	233
Roman Catholic	primary	1	1871	1	1873
	secondary	–	370	64	434
Jewish	primary	–	15	–	15
	secondary	–	4	1	5
Methodist	primary	29	4	–	33
	secondary	–	–	–	–
Other	primary	47	21	–	68
	secondary	115	48	–	163
	All voluntary schools				7621

Source: Table A12/87, DES Statistics of Education (Schools), 1987.

How far do voluntary schools of all kinds in fact offer a distinctively 'religious' form of education? Even among the aided schools, considerable differences can be found.

Church of England aided schools, like the Church itself, are varied in their practice. They are widely distributed geographically across the maintained education system. In many dioceses, the policy is to work in partnership with the local education authority, and as far as possible to play the part of a local school in a particular area.[20] In other words, children living near the school are admitted without any requirement as to religious affiliation, though parents are informed of the special religious orientation of the school. Occasionally local patterns of residence may result in a pupil roll of a majority of Muslim children attending a Church of England voluntary aided or voluntary controlled school.[21] In areas of a more mixed population, but with few voluntary aided schools, while the majority of the pupils on roll at such schools may live locally, some will have been admitted by special request of their parents, from a more distant part of the LEA or even from another neighbouring authority. Such families, who are exercising their right to require a denominationally oriented religious education for their child, will probably be required to produce supporting evidence of their church membership, for example a letter from their vicar.

For those Church of England voluntary schools which, as a matter of diocesan policy, work closely with the local education authority, there is likely to be considerably more interaction between the school and the LEA's education department than between school and diocesan board. LEA advisers will be more frequent visitors to the school than the diocesan adviser; in-service training will be arranged via the LEA; the headteacher will attend meetings with headteachers of county schools and if any restructuring of the local education system takes place, the Church of England voluntary aided school is likely to fall in with LEA proposals. However, it is always open to the governors of a voluntary aided school to exercise their right of autonomy, and refuse to comply with LEA suggestions about, for example, amalgamation of a first and middle school, or a limitation on the pupil roll. In Catholic schools this right is more frequently exercised than in Church of England schools.

Catholic voluntary aided schools,[22] like those of the Church of England, are administered on a diocesan basis, but these schools can be perceived as part of a nation-wide opportunity for Catholic children to attend Catholic schools. About two-thirds of baptized Catholic children do so. In the secondary schools 65 per cent of the teachers are themselves Catholics and in the primary schools over 90 per cent. The majority of these Catholic teachers are lay rather than members of religious orders, and this proportion has strengthened in the later years of the twentieth century (Cunningham, 1987). The aims of Catholic education are laid down on a world-wide basis and disseminated in Britain by the Catholic Truth Society, publishers to the Holy See. In all countries where Catholic

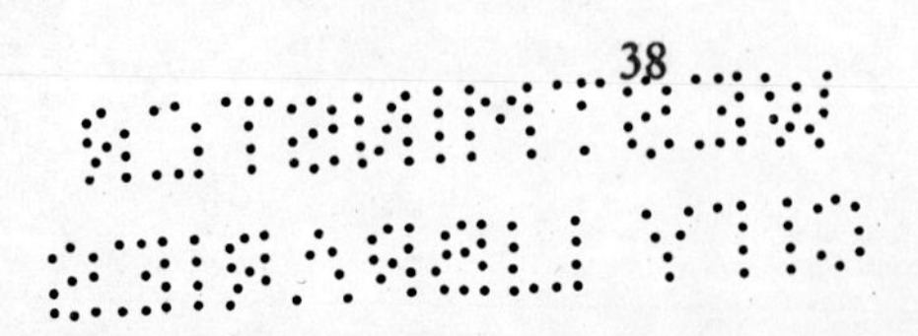

schools are provided, the aim is that through them the local Church shall evangelize, educate and contribute to 'the formation of a healthy and morally sound life-style among its members' (Congregation for Catholic Education, 1988, p. 16). In some countries there are a large number of students in Catholic schools who are not Catholics. However in the Catholic voluntary schools of England and Wales the presumption is that the first priority of the school is to serve Catholic families of the area. For example, the 1990 entry criteria for a Catholic girls high school in London[23] state that 'the school is open to Catholic families living in the borough and the surrounding boroughs, who have a commitment to their parish community. A priest's reference is always required . . . The governors are committed to taking girls from the full range of ability and will adhere to the formula for balance drawn up by the Borough unless this would involve turning down Catholic children who live there'.

Although no unqualified general statement can be made about the extent to which voluntary schools in England provide a specifically religious education, it is broadly true to say that Jewish and Catholic schools are strongly faith-linked in their policies and practice, and admit pupils whose families have a proven affiliation to those faiths. While some Church of England schools are equally doctrinaire, the majority of Church of England schools and also the Methodist schools[24] promote Christianity in all its forms and in some cases appear to be multi-faith in their practice. The festivals of the Church's year are celebrated in Church of England schools, but the festivals of other faiths are also celebrated and religious tolerance strongly encouraged.

The 1988 Education Reform Act, as we have seen, requires county schools to place emphasis on Christianity in their collective worship and in the agreed syllabus. These requirements could indirectly affect voluntary schools of Christian foundation, decreasing any inhibitions they may have felt about the single-minded promotion of the Christian religion within a multi-faith society. Nevertheless Church of England schools have been urged by the Archbishop of Canterbury's Commission on Urban Priority Areas (1985) to ensure that their student body reflects the ethnic and religious diversity present in the area, with consequent implications for the need to nurture children of other faiths within the schools (Archbishop of Canterbury's Commission on Urban Priority Areas, 1985, ch. 13). The Catholic Church also explicitly acknowledges its respect for the religious freedom and personal

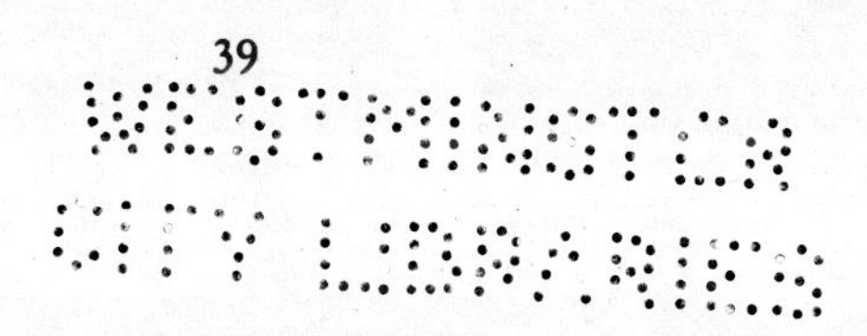

conscience of individual students and their families, but affirms that 'a Catholic school cannot relinquish its own freedom to proclaim the Gospel and to offer a formation based on the values to be found in a Christian education; this is its right and duty' (Congregation for Catholic Education, 1988, p. 5). For the voluntary school, the requirements of church and state are always to some degree in tension.

INDEPENDENT SCHOOLS

What of the private schools? Are they religious in their orientation? Certainly a great many of them claim to be Christian in tradition and atmosphere (ISIS, 1987, p. 33). Gay (1985) found that private schools of this kind had usually been established by devout individuals or particular religious orders. Schools which claimed Anglican allegiance had no links with the synodical and decision apparatus of the Church of England, nor were they backed by a diocesan infrastructure, like the voluntary schools of the maintained sector. The Church of England had no system of religious accreditation or approved list of private schools. Nevertheless it had a considerable involvement with the private sector. In England at least 114,000 pupils, at the time of Gay's research, were educated in independent senior schools claiming Anglican allegiance. Traditionally, these schools' pupils had been an important source of clergy recruitment, though this was a decreasing trend in the mid-1980s. However, many of the boys' schools employed ordained clergy as school chaplains, and their governing bodies were crowded with bishops (Gay, 1985). *Faith in the City* (Archbishop of Canterbury's Commission on Urban Priority Areas, 1985, para. 13.87) suggests that many bishops spend 'a disproportionate amount of their time at the schools attended by 6% of the population . . . and rarely visit the schools which educate the other 94%'. It asks them to examine the use of their time in this respect.

As Table 2.1 showed, the great majority of voluntary schools in the state sector are for the primary age-range. At the secondary stage, it can be said that private schools make a more significant contribution than the maintained sector to explicitly religious education. Alongside the many schools with Anglican affiliations, the Quakers and the Methodists have made a substantial investment in independent secondary education, in both cases on a residential basis. Methodist boarding schools appear to make up the most

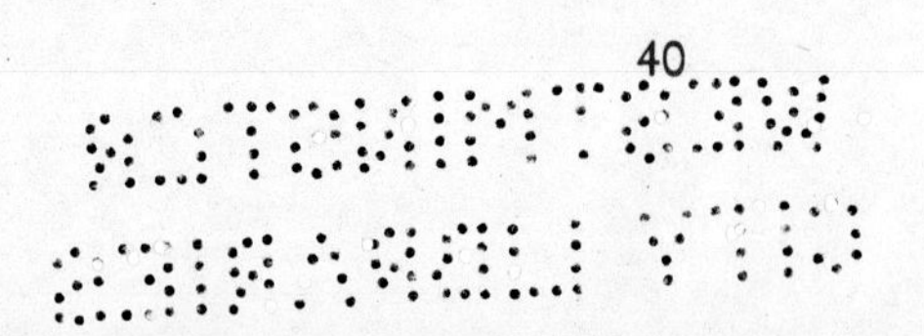

coherently organised group of 'church' schools in the independent sector. They are administered by the Board of Management for Methodist Residential Schools on behalf of the Conference of the Methodist Church (Roebuck, 1986). Representatives from each of the schools sit on the Board, and the Board Secretary is an ex-officio member of each governing body. The Quaker boarding schools, for their part, are affiliated to the Friends Schools Joint Council, but have no formally agreed common policy. In line with Quakerism's preference for small decision-making groups, each school relates to a separate responsible body of the Society of Friends which appoints its own committee of management.

In addition there is a small but important group of private schools which meet the religious needs of particular communities in a way which has no counterpart in the maintained sector. These relatively recently established religious independent schools cater in some cases for Christian minority groups, in others for minority Jewish sects, or, increasingly, for Muslim children. These schools remain in the fee-paying private sector, but are far from affluent.[25] They widen the scope of parental choice so far as religiously oriented education is concerned, but in some cases find it difficult to meet the requirements of HMI upon which their approved registration depends.[26]

During the late 1980s several of these religious groups, and in particular Muslims, have tried to obtain voluntary aided status for their schools, but at the time of writing none has been successful. The various Islamic groups base their arguments, in part, on numbers. Muslims greatly outnumber the Jewish population in England and Wales, and Muslim non-entitlement to voluntary aided schools is, they claim, purely an accident of history, since had they been equally numerous in 1944 they would surely, like the Jewish communities of the time, have been granted their own voluntary aided schools by the 1944 Education Act. A counter argument has been that to bring Muslim schools into the maintained sector as voluntary aided schools would be to incorporate a racially divisive element into public education, since a very high proportion of Muslims are of Asian origin. The Swann Report (Committee of Inquiry into the Education of Children from Ethnic Minority Groups, 1985) was opposed to such ethnically separate education.[27]

Residential or non-residential education

The great majority of both state and private schools are non-residential. In the maintained sector in 1987, 99 per cent of school pupils attended day schools. Residential (or 'boarding') education is not an expanding facility in England and Wales but it is to be found both in the maintained sector and, to a more substantial extent, in the private schools. Until the 1944 Education Act, boarding schools and private education were virtually synonymous, although many of the popular direct grant schools, part of the private sector, were day schools. The Fleming committee, reporting in 1944 (Board of Education, 1944) made one of several attempts to bring the boys' private boarding schools (the 'public schools')[28] into the maintained sector. One reason for wishing to acquire the private boarding schools was in order to take over some of the most prestigious and valuable assets of the private sector, on behalf of public education. Another reason, more specific to the residential places which the public schools provided, was so that children might learn self-dependence, at a distance from the values of the working class home.[29] A populist desire for boarding education for children was held to exist among ordinary families, but this had not been empirically tested. However, the Fleming Report's proposals met with firm resistance from the schools concerned, and were not pursued. Instead, the 1944 Education Act enjoined local authorities to provide boarding schools and boarding places within the maintained sector.[30]

In the late 1960s a further abortive attempt was made to integrate the private boarding schools into the maintained sector. The *First Report of the Public Schools Commission* (Public Schools Commission, 1968) proposed two alternative schemes of absorption, but one member of the Commission[31] contested whether the postulated demand for 27,000 additional boarding places from previously non-boarding families actually existed. In any event, the schools concerned would have nothing to do with either scheme, and no attempt at compulsion was made (Johnson, 1987, p. 17).

The public schools and their boarding facilities remained firmly part of fee-paying private education, but meanwhile a number of maintained boarding schools had been established. Provision must be counted in terms of places rather than schools, since some mainly day schools have boarding places, and vice versa. In the early 1980s there were about 10,000 boarding places in the maintained sector, but some 130,000 in the private schools (Dennison, 1984, p. 75).

However by 1987, DES statistics show that only 6,810 pupils had boarding places in the maintained sector.

The private schools are still the principal providers of boarding education, although here too numbers of boarding pupils had declined to just over 123,000 by 1989. Fewer boys have been joining boarding schools, but rather more girls. Weekly boarding is becoming more of a feature. A number of reasons for these shifting trends can be suggested, but a principal reason for the overall decline in boarding places is undoubtedly their high cost. Several interest groups, including the Boarding Schools Association, have lobbied for the extension of the Assisted Places scheme to include a boarding element, but there are no signs that the public funding of residential places at private schools will become part of education policy for the foreseeable future. Public money *is* spent to meet 'boarding need', however, principally by the Ministry of Defence and the Foreign and Commonwealth Office, on behalf of armed services and diplomatic services personnel. These and other arrangements for enabling choice of residential education are discussed in a later section of this chapter.

Single-sex or coeducation

Like residential schooling, single-sex education is to be had in both state and private schools, but is more a feature of the private than of the public sector. However, the history of this development is different from that of boarding education.

Private schools, for children of all age groups, have traditionally educated boys and girls separately. (The fees at boys' schools have always been higher than those at girls' schools, and on the whole this reflects their relative prestige in the world of private education.)

In the maintained sector, secondary education was also on a single-sex basis, in almost all schools during the first half of the twentieth century. Most infant schooling (ages 5 to 8) in the public sector was, however, coeducational from the time of the 1870 Education Act, and in some cases boys and girls were taught together throughout the elementary stage. When public education was reorganized into primary and secondary sectors by the 1944 Education Act almost all primary schools, both county and voluntary, became coeducational, and the great majority of new secondary schools also admitted both boys and girls.[32] Later, when secondary education was reorganized on comprehensive lines in most authorities (in the 1970s) many amalgamations took place with the result that, from age 5 to 18, most state schooling is now coeducational. In 1987, 94 per cent of all maintained school pupils were in mixed-sex schools. Nevertheless there are still some county secondary schools and rather more voluntary schools which are for boys or girls only. Many of the Catholic voluntary aided secondary schools are organized on this basis.

Private schools have also taken some steps in the direction of coeducation. An increasing number of preparatory schools admits both boys and girls. Many of the boys' senior schools accept girls into the sixth form, and there have been some suggested amalgamations of boys' with girls' schools. There is, however, considerable resistance to this trend from the girls' schools, many of which are 'all-through' (ages 5 to 18) in their provision. As one headmistress pointed out in the mid-1980s, while it might be fashionable for girls to move to boys' schools at 16 plus, there was no sign of its becoming fashionable for boys to join the sixth form of girls' schools (Johnson, 1987, p. 68). Takeover, rather than amalgamation, could be expected to be the experience of a girls' school joining a boys' school.

Those schools in the private sector that are coeducational argue for this on educational grounds, and these arguments would have the support of most coeducational schools in the public sector. However there is a counter-argument that girls' educational achievements and aspirations have been shown to be muted in a coeducational environment (Steedman, 1983; Bone, 1983). Another argument for single-sex education is cultural rather than purely educational. Several religious groups prefer their young people to be educated in single-sex schools, at least until their late teens. For Muslim girls this is a requirement. These religiously based preferences are probably one of the main reasons for the continued existence of some single-sex secondary schools in the maintained sector, and for the continuing popularity of girls' private schools. At the primary stage, however, coeducation seems to have won the day in state schools, and in private preparatory schools the separate education of boys and girls seems to be more a matter of tradition than principle.[33]

All-through or age-divided education

Most pupils receive their education at a series of separate schools, each of which caters for a fairly narrow age-band. The small group most likely to receive their schooling in one all-through institution are girls who attend single-sex independent schools, many of which educate girls from age 5 to 18. The choice between all-through or age-related schooling might not be worth discussing on a nationwide basis, were it not for the considerable local variation between the ages at which pupils move from one school to another, and the marked division of opinion and practice about the appropriate education of 16 to 19-year-olds. Some secondary schools are all-through in the sense of retaining this age group. In other cases, or other authorities, post-compulsory education for the 16 plus age group is in completely separate institutions such as sixth form colleges, tertiary colleges or colleges of higher education.

The variety of ages at which children may enter various schools begins at the nursery stage. In areas where there is no undue population pressure, maintained primary schools accept children who are Rising Five or even younger into a full-time reception class.[34] Alternatively, there may be half-day nursery schooling provided for some children on the premises of first or junior schools. A third possibility for the pre-schoolchild, still within the remit of the local authority, is a separate nursery school. The only common requirement is that by the age of 5 the child must be attending, or transfer to, a full-time class in a school which also educates older children (to the ages of 7 or 8).

So far as the private sector is concerned, defined for this pre-school discussion as anywhere where payment is made for under-five care and education,[35] variety is infinite, ranging from voluntary groups staffed mainly by mothers, where only the hire of a hall is paid for, to costly, elaborately uniformed, classes of toddlers in private pre-preparatory schools. Some private schools accept children at two and a half years of age explicitly to scoop the pool, in the hope that parents will not subsequently think it worth the disruption of moving their child to another, perhaps initially preferred, school when they reach that school's admission age, which may be at 3 or 4 (Johnson, 1987).

Continuing with the private sector, the main divisions are pre-prep (to age 7), preparatory to age 11 or 13 (the latter especially in the case of traditional boys' schools where Common Entrance is sat) and senior from 11 or 13 to age 18 or 19. For girls, as we have already seen, there are some all-through schools with junior and senior departments spanning the ages 5 to 18, but other girls' private schools tend to break at 11 rather than 13. Most senior private schools have sixth forms, retaining the majority of pupils to age 18.

A number of boys' schools have coeducational sixth form education.

In maintained education, the principal division is between primary and secondary schooling. Primary education runs from 5 (or Rising Five) to 11 or 12, in infant and junior or first and middle schools. During their primary years, most children attend two schools which are administratively and socially quite separate, although they may be geographically close to one another.

To complicate the issue further, some middle schools are 'deemed secondary'. Most of these schools retain pupils to the age of 13. The more common secondary age range is from 11 (or 12) to 16, when compulsory schooling ends but when a proportion of pupils continue their education to age 18 or 19, either in the same school or in one of the separate post-compulsory institutions referred to earlier.

Because of local government reorganization over the years, amalgamating authorities that had different traditions about the age of school transfer, a single county may comprise several districts where different traditions still prevail. Hertfordshire is an example here, having first and middle schools in some areas which were previously part of Bedfordshire and infant and junior schools in other parts of the county. Adjoining smaller local authorities may also organize their schools on different lines. For example in the borough of Harrow children change school at 8 and 12, whereas in Hillingdon, an adjacent outer London borough, they transfer at 7 and 11.

The significance of all this variety for parental choice is, first, that choice has to be exercised on a number of occasions, and secondly that across-the-border choice (whether between divisions of a county or between juxtaposed smaller authorities) poses considerable administrative problems.

Disregarding for the moment families who use both public and private education for their children, parents who stay with the maintained sector can express a choice for a particular school on at least three occasions: when the child first enters full-time education, at the upper primary stage and again when secondary education begins. In the debate about parental choice most attention has focused on the move from primary to secondary school. However, many parents find that lower and upper primary schools, although sharing the same name or the same site, are quite separate institutions with a sharply different ethos. Since the child will in any case be experiencing a marked change of school style, parents may think it appropriate to express a preference for a quite unconnected junior or middle school for the upper primary stage. Then at the secondary stage, parents may, for example, prefer a transfer age of 11 to that of 12, and may seek to transfer their children at the end of Year 11 in a middle school to a secondary school in a nearby area that accepts pupils at that age, leaving Year 12 of the middle school depleted in numbers and resources for the final year of primary education.

Similar problems are presented when parents move their children between state and private schools, or vice versa, at various points in their education. The main point to note is that the exercise of parental choice is not a once-for-all affair in the school life of each child. It requires repeated decision-making by parents, and considerable flexibility of all age-related institutions.

Even with the case of all-through schools, however, pupils do not necessarily stay the entire course. Fee-paying pupil numbers may be sharply depleted at sixth form level (a stage at which fees commonly rise), as parents take the opportunity to choose another institution for the post-compulsory years.

The question of whether education *should* be all-through or age-divided has never been more hotly argued than in respect of post-compulsory schooling. Ranson (1990) takes the 16 plus issue as his prime example of controversy, when discussing the politics of school reorganization. For our purposes it is sufficient to note that for good or ill 16 plus is now, for those young people who continue their education, potentially a watershed of change. Even if their secondary school has a sixth form, which is far from always the case, many different educational paths may be taken. This is a stage at which student choice, as well as parental choice, may be influential. Post-sixteen education is not compulsory, so numbers in any case fall off at this stage, with the result that the different institutions, both within and across the public and private sectors, are in competition for the same relatively small cohort of individuals.

Institutional or home-based education

Parents' rights to choose their children's education include the right to educate them outside the school system altogether. It has been pointed out (Education Otherwise, 1985) that the term 'compulsory school age' is misleading. It is education, rather than schooling, which is compulsory, from the fifth to the sixteenth birthday.[36] Parents of children in this compulsory age range are required to ensure that they receive 'efficient full-time education suitable to [their] age, ability and aptitude, either by regular attendance at school or otherwise' (Education Act 1944, s. 36).

The two principal organizations in Britain which provide support for parents choosing home-based education for their children are Education Otherwise (EO) – which takes its name from the section of the 1944 Act quoted above – and the World-wide Education Service (WES). The aims and operations of these two concerns differ.

WES is part of the Parents' National Education Union (PNEU), founded in the last decade of the nineteenth century, and fulfils a number of educational functions throughout the world.[37] WES has no government grants but is run as a business with charitable status. The relevance of the organization for this discussion is that it provides a Home School service for parents wishing to educate their children at home. Fees are charged to cover the 'distance learning' materials and tutorial support, so in one sense the Home School scheme can be seen as a private school at home. Local education authorities occasionally use the scheme for children who are out of school for various reasons. This practice can be linked with the payment of independent school fees by LEAs, to be discussed in a later section.

Many families who use the Home School service do so during a period of time overseas. The scheme is geared to minimize any difficulty the child might experience in re-settling into a UK school, either in the state or the private sector. Parents living in the United Kingdom who enrol for the WES' Home School service usually do so because they believe their child will benefit from an approach different from that of school-based education. The Home School scheme is not a correspondence course, however. It relies on parents or other adults using the Home School materials to *teach* the child, and expects enrolled families to follow a regular daily timetable and make use of the scheme's assessment system at the end of each term. In undertaking this work parents have the support of contact with a personal tutor who is a qualified and experienced teacher. The ethos of the WES is not a de-schooling one, but rather it seeks to capitalize on the commitment and involvement of parents in their child's education when circumstances require that this take place out of school.

Education Otherwise, by contrast, is a decentralized voluntary association (with charitable status) which affirms that parents have the primary responsibility for their children's education and that they have the right to exercise this responsibility by educating them out of school. The association is not committed to any particular *system* of education, and does not provide teaching syllabuses and materials. It depends on the participation and mutual support of members to help parents establish what is best suited to the needs of their own children and their own beliefs, and to provide a network for communication and debate. The association's guide to home-based education points out that 'members of EO do not necessarily have strongly-rooted antipathy to schools, but most wish to take back responsibility from the State for the education of their children, partly because their concern and care as parents will provide a basis for a better education, but also because home education adds an immensely valuable and enjoyable dimension to their family lives' (Education Otherwise, 1985, p. 4).

The guide includes a discussion of the law relating to the education of children out of school, and addresses the question of the relationship of the EO family with the LEA. On the cost of home education, the guide suggests that 'the main cost of home education is loss of earnings and perhaps career prospects on the part of one parent. Generally, direct expenditure on home education is very modest – negligible in comparison with the cost of even the cheapest private education; and there are of course some financial savings in not sending a child to school' (Education Otherwise, 1985, p. 16). For most members of EO, the practice of home education seems to be undertaken following an unsatisfactory school experience, either of their own or of their child.

Some 2,000 families or groups are on the contact list of Education Otherwise. In an average year, the association knows of roughly 1,000 school age children who are not at school. However, on a nation-wide basis the number of children in the United Kingdom not on the roll of any school is one of the great unknowns of education statistics. LEAs have a record of children excluded from or transferred from school for a variety of reasons who are on the roll of an LEA 'Home Tuition' centre (although actual attendance at these centres is not always closely monitored (Bird *et al.*, 1981)). However, the number of children who never join a school in the first place may be far greater. The existence of these children will not necessarily be known to the LEA (Johnson, 1987). Education Otherwise suggests a form of words by which parents intending to educate their children at home might notify the LEA of this, but they point out that it is not obligatory to do so. And there may be many families who neither send their children to school nor make themselves known to any home-centred support service such as those discussed here.

How are parents helped or hindered in making choices? So far we have discussed some of the variety that exists in education. Apart from the possibility of educating children at home, there are schools which are public or private, free or fee-paying, selective or non-selective, day or boarding, coeducational or single-sex, all-through or age-related. Only the opportunity for an entirely secular schooling is missing, since from the purist point of view neither maintained, voluntary nor independent schools offer a fully secular education.

To spell out all this variety is not necessarily to say that equal opportunities of choice exist for all these forms of schooling. In some sparsely populated areas the variety of provision so far described is almost completely lacking. There are so few schools that the idea of choice may seem a mockery. But even where variety exists, the exercise of choice requires some administrative procedures. The remaining sections of this chapter examine some of the arrangements for expression of preference, admission policies, appeals and waiting lists which regulate entry to county and voluntary schools, together with the positive steps which these schools take to recruit pupils. Finally we look at the recruitment of pupils to independent schools and the circumstances in which public money is available for the payment of independent school fees.

Choosing a maintained school

The 1988 Reform Act has altered some of the 1980 Education Act's ground rules for LEAs, in their management of parental choice. As we have seen (chapter 1) they must respond to parental demand for places at a particular school by admitting children up to the limits of the school's physical capacity. But it is still the 1980 Education Act which governs some aspects of parents' right of choice. For example the act clarified the position of parents who applied for their child to be educated in a school outside the local authority in which they lived. Such an application had to be treated by the 'host' LEA in the same way as a preference expressed by a parent living in the authority. This formalization of cross-border parental choice was an important new development. The 1980 Act also required LEAs to publish full details of their admission policy arrangements, including arrangements made on a cross-border basis. The form of publication was subject to regulations made by the secretary of state (The Education (School Information) Regulations 1981, S.I. 1981 No. 630). Later in the decade, the 1986 Education (No. 2) Act (s. 33) further required LEAs and governing bodies of schools to consult each other once a year about the satisfactory nature, or otherwise, of admission procedures, and any proposed changes to these. This applied to the governing bodies of both county and voluntary schools.

LEAs also have to publish details of their arrangements for appeals against admission decisions. Schedule 2 of the 1980 Education Act lays down requirements for the constitution of appeal committees. These cover not only LEAs, regarding admission decisions about county or voluntary controlled schools, but also the governors of aided or special agreement schools who control their own admissions. The procedures to be followed by both kinds of committee are identical. Only their constitution is slightly different. Decisions of the appeal committee are binding on the LEA or governors of the voluntary school concerned.

CHOOSING A VOLUNTARY AIDED SCHOOL

Although the terms of the 1980 and 1986 Education Acts apply to voluntary aided as to all other maintained schools, there is one important difference in their position. Voluntary aided schools devise their own admissions policy, and it is the governors of the school who operate that policy. An important effect of the 1980 Act was to require governors to clarify that policy, or in some cases to formulate a policy for the first time.[38]

Since voluntary aided schools control their own admissions, it is within their power to maintain waiting lists, and some do so. Schools most likely to follow this practice are those which are strongly faith-linked in their admissions policy, i.e. the Catholic and certain orthodox Jewish schools. In county schools the main intakes of pupils are administered by the LEA, and it is only when parents wish to transfer their child from another area, or another school, part-way through the primary or secondary phase, that waiting list procedures are likely to be operated by the school.

All these arrangements for expression of preference, admission policies, appeals and waiting lists, become less salient at a time of falling rolls, but voluntary schools in particular may find themselves 'oversubscribed' even when the age cohort of pupils is not creating any general pressure for places. The 1986 Act's requirement for governing bodies and LEA to consult each other annually about admission procedures was no doubt intended to keep aided schools' governors' policies broadly in line with those operating in county schools. Some authorities were using falling rolls, and the expression of parental choice, to determine their school closure proposals for the county schools. Other authorities took the view that the 'efficient use of resources' required them to manage admissions so as to keep the maximum number of schools viable, their rolls being artificially controlled by LEA edict rather than by parental preference. Following the 1988 Reform Act, however, schools with low enrolment can no longer be protected by enrolment being restricted at other more popular schools. Where demand exists, both county and voluntary schools must admit pupils up to the limits of the school's physical capacity. Less popular schools may decide to respond with new marketing or 'reputation management' strategies, as some have already done in areas of low juvenile population. Ways in which schools in the maintained sector handle the recruitment of pupils are further discussed below.

RECRUITMENT OF PUPILS TO MAINTAINED SECTOR SCHOOLS

Information about maintained schools, and opportunities to visit the schools have tended to be provided more as a service to the local community rather than as a deliberate attempt to enlist pupils to particular schools. The 1980 Education Act requires local authorities to prepare general information about all their schools, and to make this available on request. Schools too have to provide certain information about curriculum, pastoral care, discipline, school dress and several other matters, including particulars about arrangements for parents to visit the school when they are considering sending their child there (Schedule 2, 1981 School Information Regulations). These details are usually published by the LEA in booklet form, and are available to interested parents at the schools concerned. Some schools have prepared additional information which they distribute as a supplement to the 'official' booklet. A small study of school information booklets (Muskett, 1986) found, however, that schools producing friendly, interesting booklets which were not difficult to read, tended to omit some of the basic information needed by parents who are choosing a school. The schools which included most of the statutorily required information tended to produce dull, difficult to read booklets. Muskett suggests that many schools have a long way to go to achieve both high information content and a readable, friendly style.

The main public relations exercise of maintained schools, concerned with the recruitment of pupils, is the open evening or open day, when families come by invitation or in response to public notices to visit the school premises and view the work displayed. Staff are in attendance, and in the case of secondary schools, families may be shown round by pupil 'guides'. These events, which have become routine for most schools, are informal if crowded occasions, usually lasting for several hours, and not timetabled to include formal presentations by the headteacher or other staff. At the secondary stage the open evenings at local schools are all held in the autumn term, before parents of final-year primary school children have to decide on their transfer preference for the following academic year. At the primary stage, LEAs may operate several intake dates, depending on the birth date of the child, but the opportunity to visit the schools usually comes early in the preceding academic year.

The open evening is an anonymous occasion, when only those families who already have children at the school are identifiable to staff, unless parents make a particular point of introducing themselves. In the early days of falling rolls schools in the maintained sector tended not to target their marketing exercises, preferring to avoid any impression of 'poaching' parents whose children might otherwise join the roll of some other schools. However, the idea of reputation management is beginning to emerge as a necessary strategy for the maintained school whose potential clients, the parents, are finding their position strengthened by government education policy. Headteachers in a small sample contacted by the Open University in 1987 laid stress on supplying positive information, encouraging access, involvement with the community, public appearances and fostering good standards as their main tactics in reputation management (Johnson, Whitaker and Kay, 1988). Dennison (1989) emphasizes the impression that outsiders receive of the school as vital to its 'competitive edge'. Seminars at which headteachers are helped to identify and promote their school's chief 'selling point' have proved popular. Greenall

(1988) suggests that public relations policies, for schools as for other organizations, have long-term benefits. The full effects of parental choice, falling rolls and reduced funding may not be felt for some time. But those schools that will fare best in the new competitive environment, Greenall considers, are those which have been taking the need for good public relations seriously for some years, and have 'nurtured' their reputation rather than allowing it to be built up by the haphazard impressions of those outside the school.

Choosing an independent school

Independent schools of various kinds are part of the range of education about which parental choice may be exercised. Some reference has already been made to the admission procedures followed in academically selective independent schools. This section will examine ways in which independent schools recruit their pupils and the sources of financial help with fees to which parents may have access.

RECRUITMENT OF PUPILS TO INDEPENDENT SCHOOLS

This is a more self-conscious process than the maintained sector procedures already discussed. Independent schools do not have the LEA infrastructure which handles the placement of children in maintained schools. Nor are they bound by the requirements of the 1980 Education Act and its regulations regarding the publication of information. These apply only to maintained schools. However, it could be said that the statutory requirements are to some extent a copy of practices already followed by independent schools.

Individual private schools maintain regularly updated glossy brochures which they issue to interested parents. These brochures provide at least as much information as maintained schools are required to supply, and may also go into considerable detail about school amenities, the qualifications of staff, examination pass rates, destinations of school leavers and so on. Another purpose of these documents is to convey something of the particular *raison d'etre* of the school. The independent sector of education has no overarching corporate existence. Some independent school heads recognize a common purpose with certain other independent schools, but most see their own school as a unique unit which must justify its continuing existence by making clear what the school stands for (Johnson, 1987). The headmaster of a long-established independent school for boys remarked that revising the school brochure so that it clearly conveyed his aims for the school was his first priority task after taking up his post. This emphasis on the *raison d'etre* of the independent school is perhaps the equivalent of the search for a 'selling point' which some maintained school heads are now undertaking.

The parent who receives an independent school's brochure has already had to take the initiative in approaching the school, as indeed they would have to do in order to obtain the information available from a maintained school. To attract parental attention to private schooling in the first place, a number of tactics are used. Many independent schools are affiliated to the Independent Schools Information Service. An annual ISIS publication 'Choosing Your Independent School' is widely advertised. It lists and briefly describes all the affiliated schools (over 1,300), and gives contact telephone numbers and addresses for all the schools. Apart from setting out the range of schools available, the book suggests questions which the family needs to decide before narrowing their choice to particular schools (boarding or day, single-sex or coeducational, academic or less academic). It also advises parents on what to look out for when making exploratory visits to schools: what the fees and any supplementary costs of attending the school are, the appearance and behaviour of the pupils, whether the head asks for information about the child in question, the school's rules and forms of contact with parents, the range of the curriculum and examinations pupils are prepared for, class size and the stability and quality of teaching staff.

ISIS issues regular press releases on matters pertaining to private education,[39] and regional branches of ISIS have for many years provided information stalls at County Shows and other venues. A recent innovation is a national independent schools exhibition. Although independent schools, even those affiliated with ISIS, do not make up an organized independent 'sector', they benefit from the existence of their publicity arm ISIS, which gives them far more favourable exposure than the giant maintained sector tends to receive. The divided responsibilities of the DES and the local authorities mean that it is in neither's interest to take on the task of promoting the sector as a whole. It remains to be seen what strategies grant-maintained schools pursue to promote their image, and whether they seek to organize some coordinated publicity.

As a publicity initiative of their own, independent schools, like maintained schools, have regular Open Days, and these are advertised in the local and (where appropriate) the national press. A less obvious but perhaps more influential investment of effort is made in the reception and treatment of families who approach a school individually. Even in popular and well established independent schools headteachers dedicate considerable time to the reception of interested parents, a task to which they give high priority. Even though the school may be oversubscribed at the present time, there can be no guarantee that the flow of applications will continue without appropriate encouragement. By contrast, in the maintained sector even in a time of falling rolls there has been a tendency for oversubscription to be seen as an administrative headache rather than a potential resource for survival. At one Scottish maintained school which benefited from new parental choice procedures, receiving an unprecedented number of applications, the headteacher remarked that the pressure on the school was an embarrassment. If parents actually came to look at the school before registering their preference, the caretaker showed them round (Wilby, 1988). Some increased enthusiasm for the recruitment of pupils to maintained schools may however follow the introduction of LMS, as part of the 1988 Reform Act. At least 75 per cent of each school's budget will be calculated on a per capita basis, so the supply of pupils may be seen in a new light.

The use of public money to help pay independent school fees

The positive approach taken by independent schools to pupil recruitment has to grapple not only with the general decline in the size of the school-age population – a factor also experienced by maintained schools – but also the financial cost to the parent of using private education.

It is often claimed that private education is 'subsidized' by the granting of charitable status to certain independent schools. This is a complex and politically contentious issue which cannot be adequately explored here (useful sources are Rogers, 1980; Pring, 1982; Salter and Tapper, 1985). Quite apart from the possible 'subsidy' provided by charitable status there are a number of clearcut ways in which public money is used to help parents pay private school fees. The three main mechanisms are: boarding school allowances, payable because of family mobility required by public sector employment; DES funded places at independent schools specializing in music and dance; and the Assisted Places scheme introduced in the 1980 Education Act.

BOARDING SCHOOL ALLOWANCES

These allowances are funded from the Defence Vote. Service families may claim such an allowance for the residential education of their children whether or not the family is posted overseas, provided they declare themselves to be 'mobile', that is, prepared to move house to follow the posting of the service member. The principle for payment of the allowance is to provide continuity of education, and may be used to pay boarding fees at either a maintained or an independent school. The allowance (between £1,100 and £1,300 per term in 1988, depending on the stage of the child's education) does not usually cover the full cost of board and tuition at an independent school, but goes a substantial way towards it. In 1988, 20,796 allowances were drawn, by 12,094 commissioned officers and 8,702 other ranks. If the child in question attends a maintained boarding school, the allowance is sufficient to meet the boarding fees. There are of course no tuition fees charged to parents of children at maintained boarding schools (although these are recouped on an inter-authority basis). But, as already noted, places at maintained boarding schools are in decline. Almost ninety per cent of service children who receive the boarding school allowance in fact attend independent schools, the allowance being augmented as necessary by payments from their parents.

Another group eligible for boarding school allowances are the children of diplomatic service personnel. These allowances, although fewer in number and total cost to the public exchequer,[40] are individually higher than those paid for Services children. The Foreign and Commonwealth Office bases these allowances directly on the fees currently charged by a sample of independent schools.[41] The principle of payment is, once again, to enable continuity of education in the face of family mobility. It is also recognized that diplomatic service families do not have access to the forces schools which service families may use on a day school basis in many overseas stations (notably West Germany). Many diplomatic postings are in the equivalent of the forces' 'Extra

Command Areas', that is, where the staff maintained are few in number, insufficient to justify the creation of a school. Moreover, it is considered that most diplomatic families have to use boarding education for their children from an early age (rather than mainly during the secondary stage, as is the case for many service families). Almost all junior age residential places are in boarding schools of the independent sector, and the diplomatic services boarding school allowance takes due account of this.

The boarding school allowances described here come directly from central government funds and do not involve the local authority from which the family originates (although that authority will be required to contribute to the No Area Pool from which tuition costs of places at maintained boarding schools are met). There are certain other circumstances in which 'boarding need' is recognized and payments made on behalf of a local child by the LEA. Local authorities acknowledge the criteria for boarding need outlined in the Martin Report:

> (i) Cases in which both parents are abroad;
> (ii) Cases in which the parents are in England or Wales, but liable to frequent moves from one area to another;
> (iii) Cases in which home circumstances are seriously prejudicial to the normal development of the child;
> (iv) Cases in which a special aptitude in the child requires special training which can be given to the child only by means of a boarding education.
>
> (Ministry of Education, 1960, para. 10)

However, the award of an allowance for boarding need based on these criteria is a discretionary matter for the LEA, and the allowances tend to be few in number. Moreover, the allowance made may meet only part of the cost of the boarding place. Families awarded an allowance because of boarding need may be unable to meet the remaining cost, and have to relinquish the boarding place. Unlike the identification of statemented special educational need,[42] the recognition of boarding need does not statutorily trigger LEA payment of the full cost of meeting that need, whether in an independent or a maintained school. It is for this reason (among others) that the Boarding Schools Association, together with other interest groups, has campaigned for a boarding element to be included in the Assisted Places scheme, but in the foreseeable future this development seems unlikely.

DES PLACES AT SCHOOLS FOR MUSIC AND DANCE

The award of these places at specialized independent schools for talented children is of long standing, but the commitment of public money is extremely small, compared with that for Services boarding education.[43] There is no question of 'eligibility' for a DES place. A finite number of places (509 in the school year 1988/9) are funded at particular schools, and these places are competed for. Moreover, they are subject to means testing.

These 'special talent' places can be seen as the residue of earlier arrangements which allowed able children from the maintained sector to take up free places in fee-paying schools. The 1976 Education Act put an end to this general arrangement, but the special arrangements regarding schools for children of artistic talent were retained. Local authorities were also permitted to continue to pay the fees of selected children at such schools, without seeking the agreement of the secretary of state. Setting up maintained schools for the fostering of artistic talent is one area of educational provision that the state has not embarked on and is unlikely to undertake in the future, given the high cost of such specialized education.[44] At the time when academic selectivity in education fell out of favour in the maintained sector it still remained acceptable to select children on artistic merit. Although the DES funding of places for music and dance is a small commitment of public money, it has some symbolic importance.

THE ASSISTED PLACES SCHEME

There was a five year gap between the Direct Grant Grammar Schools (Cessation of Grant) Regulations of 1975 (under a Labour government) and the introduction, as part of the 1980 Education Act, of the Assisted Places scheme (by a Conservative government). While in some senses the new scheme can be seen as taking the place of the former direct grant arrangement, there are significant differences between the two.

The direct grant schools had played a part in the general evolution of secondary education in England and Wales during the middle decades of the twentieth century. They were fee-charging independent schools which, in 1926, elected to receive a capitation grant direct from the Board of Education on condition that a percentage of their places was awarded, without fees, to children from maintained sector elementary schools. Glennerster and Wilson

(1970) point out that the advantage of this arrangement for the direct grant schools was two-fold.

> In the first place the grant allowed the school to offer free places without financial loss; in the second it kept the fees charged for other pupils below the full economic cost. Local authorities were not limited to the number of free places financed by the grant. In some cases they paid for extra places for children from local elementary schools.
>
> (Glennerster and Wilson, 1970, p. 58)

The 1944 Education Act transformed the system of maintained education, with its aim of secondary education for all. The 'hybrid' position of the direct grant schools, tenuously linking the private and state sectors of education, became increasingly anomalous. Nevertheless, during the post-war period of rapid expansion of education, 'roofs over heads' were a prime preoccupation, and the secondary places available in direct grant schools were more than ever needed. However, as we have seen, the scheme was eventually phased out by the issue of regulations to that effect in 1975.

The cessation of the direct grant scheme was seen by some as a diminution of opportunity for able children from the maintained sector. The 1980 Education Act established a new link with the independent schools by the introduction of Assisted Places. Independent secondary schools organized on a charitable basis might enter into a participation agreement with the Secretary of State for Education, who would reimburse the schools for fees remitted to pupils selected for assisted places. The overall purpose of the scheme was to enable 'pupils who might otherwise not be able to do so to benefit from education at independent schools' (Education Act 1980, s. 17). Assisted places are means-tested, and regulations require that participating schools must offer sixty per cent of these places to pupils formerly in maintained education.

The main distinction between the direct grant and the Assisted Places schemes will be apparent. The local authority has no part to play in participative agreements under the new scheme. The award of places concerns only the secretary of state, the independent school and families who apply for a place for their child. In the early stages of the scheme if a 16 year-old from a maintained school was offered an assisted place in the sixth form of an independent school, the agreement of the local authority's education committee was needed, but a change in regulations brought this requirement to an end in 1983. The LEA now has no operational connection with the Assisted Places scheme.

By 1988 over 27,000 pupils held assisted places in independent schools participating in the scheme. Thirty-two per cent of these places were totally free, being held by children from families with an income of less than £7,258. The cost of the scheme for the 1988/89 academic year was £51 million (figures supplied by the Assisted Places Unit, DES). Some research into the early operation of the scheme has been completed. It is discussed in chapter 4.

Other sources of financial help with fees

The *public* money which directly assists families to pay school fees for private education is, it can be seen, by no means a universally available benefit. It is available only to families of low income whose child obtains the offer of an assisted place by whatever entrance procedure the school in question operates; to successful competitors for one of the few DES-funded places at schools specializing in music or dance; and for the children of families in certain forms of government service which require family mobility. Other families choosing private education are required to pay the fees themselves.[45] There are, however, two main sources of *private* assistance which help some families to meet school fees. These are the payment of children's independent school fees as part of a parent's terms of employment, and various bursary, scholarship or fee remission schemes operated by the schools themselves.

Conditions of employment which include some payments in kind or 'perks' are by no means unusual. The company car is the most widely known example. Payment of, or contribution to, independent school fees for employees' children gained popularity in the 1970s. Subsequent closing of various tax loopholes has considerably reduced the cash value of these benefits, but they are still a feature of some families' budgeting for private education.

Independent schools are largely autonomous in their financial affairs, and no general statement can be made about the incidence of fee remission or reduction in the private schools. A research enquiry has shown that many charitable funds dedicated for educational purposes are never called upon, because their existence is not known of (Fitzherbert and Eastwood, 1988). ISIS is the most accessible source of information about the independent schools affiliated to it. Most entries in their guide to independent schools

(ISIS, 1988) indicate that some scholarships and bursaries are offered, but the school itself must be approached for details. Some independent schools give fee discounts for the children of clergy, teachers or members of the armed forces. As already noted, assisted place payments under the 1980 Act's scheme do not include a boarding element, but in 1987, of 1,600 Assisted Place pupils holding boarding places, over 990 received help with boarding from the schools themselves (Assisted Places Committee, 1988). However, ISIS points out in its guide that private education is a costly business. For most families wanting to use independent schools the preferred strategy is to plan early, taking out insurance policies to cover the cost of school fees while the child is still in infancy.

Conclusion

This chapter has tackled a somewhat unwieldy task, in bringing together information and comment from a wide range of sources about some of the principal features of available education and some of the processes which help or hinder the operation of choice. Such a broad picture is necessarily superficial in its detail; some readers will already know far more about some aspects of available education than has been given here. But compiling this account serves the purpose of clarifying the educational setting in which any policy of parental choice has to operate. Parents and teachers alike need some awareness of the scope for choice which exists, and which inevitably structures the expression of preference.

But to know what is available, together with some of the administrative processes of choice, is not the same as knowing what parental choice as a policy will mean in practice. In the next two chapters we turn to the findings of recent research, to see what happens when parents take – or make – the opportunity to choose their children's schools. We begin with the maintained sector.

Chapter 3

Maintained education: research into choice

How do parents choose schools and what happens when they do? What do we know from research? As with most studies in education, research into parental choice has tended to look separately at the maintained and private sectors of education. In this chapter we focus on parental choice of maintained schools, the schools most affected by the requirements of the 1980 and 1988 Education Acts.

It could be said that parental choice, central government's 'key element of policy'[1] has been promoted as a matter of principle rather than in response to researched demand. Most of the research examining processes of parental choice has been carried out since the 1980 Education Act, which first laid emphasis on parents' right to choose their child's school. However a few studies before the 1980s came up with some findings on the exercise of parental choice, findings which were incidental to, rather than the central purpose of, the research.

Pre-1980 research into parental choice

Two research enquiries into the relationship between family and school made contact with parents in the late 1970s, and asked some questions about choosing schools. These two studies (Elliott *et al.*, 1981; Johnson and Ransom, 1983) both focused on families with children of secondary school age. Parents of primary school children, however, were the subject of an earlier and more large-scale enquiry, commissioned by the Plowden Committee to inform their report *Children and their Primary Schools* (Central Advisory Council for Education (England), 1967). A national survey, which forms part of volume 2 of the Committee's report, drew on a sample of over 3,000 parents.

The survey explored many aspects of parents' attitudes to and relationships with their children's schools. Only one question was asked about the availability of choice, but this revealed that over fifty per cent of parents considered that they did have a choice, in that there was another nearby maintained primary school which their child could have attended if they wished. The researchers' report (Central Advisory Council, 1967, vol. 2, App. 3, para. 3.8) points out that this was only the situation as parents perceived it; 'they may not have known whether in fact the local education authority would have permitted their children to attend other schools in the neighbourhood'.

Parents were also asked whether they had ever made a positive attempt to get their child into a different school by approaching the 'Education Office or anyone else in authority'. Only six per cent of parents had done so. Of these, half had obtained and one-third failed to obtain the desired school. Other cases were still pending at the time of interview (op. cit., para. 3.11).

Parents who believed they had had a choice because of the availability of other local primary schools were asked their reasons for deciding on the school their child attended.

> The reasons given most frequently . . . were, firstly, that it was the most convenient for the child to get to, it was the nearest or safest to reach or there were no main roads to cross (49% of parents who had a choice of school). Secondly came religious reasons, either that the school was chosen because it was a church school or an alternative was rejected for the same reason (30%). Thirdly, parents chose primary schools because they had heard good reports about them (24%) and, fourthly, because their other children or other relatives or friends of the sampled children were there or had been previously (23%). Seven per cent of the parents specifically mentioned that there were better educational standards in the chosen schools and six per cent that the atmosphere seemed happier and more homely and friendly.
>
> It is interesting that almost three-quarters of the children had had other relatives attending the sampled schools either at the time of the survey or previously. Sixty-two percent had, or had had, brothers or sisters there and as many as 20 per cent of the selected children's fathers or mothers had been at the same schools. (op. cit., para 3.9 and 3.10)

These are rare findings about parental choice of primary school. No national interview survey of parents on a similar scale has been carried out since 1967.

The Plowden Committee, in their own report (op. cit., vol. 1) did not comment directly on the national survey's enquiry into choice, but they took the view that 'parents must be given some choice whenever this is possible and they should have information on which to base it. They are more likely to support a school they have freely chosen, and to give it the loyalty which is so essential if their children are to do the same. Whenever a school is unpopular that should be an indication to the authority to find out why and make it better' (op. cit., vol. 1, para 120). The report puts forward as one of its formal recommendations[2] that 'Parents should be allowed to choose their children's primary school whenever this is possible. Authorities should take steps to improve schools which are shown to be consistently unpopular with parents' (op. cit., vol. 1, para 130). This is classified in the report as a recommendation 'not subject to extra expenditure or requiring changes of law or Department's Regulations'. The LEA is listed as the 'agency mainly responsible for putting the recommendation into effect'. These were very early days in the debate about enabling parental choice. Since that time, local authorities have shown that they can produce counter arguments about schools which are unpopular with parents, and put forward reasons why parental choice should not prevail, even in the face of legislation.

The opportunity, and funding, for a nation-wide approach to parents do not often occur. From a research point of view, parents are expensive to contact in person, and often hard to locate. It is easier to conduct research with parents who visit the school, rather than seek them out in their homes. As part of the SSRC Cambridge Accountability Project – a major study conducted in 1979/80 on the accountability of schools – Elliott took the opportunity of a meeting of 'new parents' at one comprehensive school to ask these parents to complete a questionnaire about their reasons for choosing the school their child had recently begun to attend. Elliott (1981a) points out that his sample is small, fortuitous and probably skewed towards the middle class. His work has, however, been influential not so much for the validity of his findings[3] as for the analysis he applied to them. He separated 'process' from 'product' criteria of choice. Parents using product criteria were those who looked towards the outcomes of schooling such as academic achievement in making their choice. Those using process criteria emphasized the way the school was run, and how this would affect their child. For Elliott's group of parents, process seemed more important than product, and this finding was further tested when Elliott subsequently asked all fourth year parents to say what they valued about their children's school, choosing from an inventory of over forty statements. Substantial support was given to these two statements:

> Children's personal and social development at school is at least as important as their academic development.
>
> The most important thing about a school is whether the children are happy and enjoy their lessons.
>
> (Elliott, 1981a, p. 57)

Elliott was the first to note what later research has often confirmed, that parents given an opportunity to record their reasons for choosing a school tend to rate highly the personal happiness of their child.

Another enquiry in the 1970s which produced some findings on parental choice was the Schools, Parents and Social Services project conducted at Brunel University from 1974 to 1977. The Department of Education and Science funded this study of the working relationships between schools, parents and a number of welfare agencies whose clients included children of secondary school age.[4] The research included home interviews with 109 parents of secondary school children (Johnson and Ransom, 1980, 1983). The approach to parents was particularly concerned to establish whether parents who rarely visited the school were in fact 'apathetic' about their children's education, as teachers surmised. Once again, questions about choice of school were incidental to rather than the central purpose of the research.

My colleagues[5] and I carried out the semi-structured interviews which formed the basis of this study in 1976/7. All the parents had children at one of four comprehensive schools which were the subject of case study.[6] The interviews explored the range of contacts which parents had with their child's present school, and before that with the primary school. Parents were also asked whether they had tried to choose the schools their children attended, and on what basis.

For the working class families living in the outer suburbs of London whom we interviewed, choice of their child's first school had not been a debated process. For most of the families, their children's primary schools were essentially local institutions, as close to home as possible, which all the neighbourhood's children in turn attended, and where the 'taking and collecting' of the early years was not too long a walk.

Again, at the change from infant to junior school[7] although there was often a clear impression – and not always a welcomed one – of a new and different school, choice did not seem to be an issue. This was where the children moved on to, and where the parents too must wend their way for concerts, sports days and other public events.

However, the move from primary to secondary education was seen by these parents as some kind of turning point in the child's life. For parents too it marked a change of role. Parents had to exercise some kind of judgement about what the future could hold for their child since they had to name several schools, in order of preference, for their child's secondary education. Our findings about the factors on which these preferences were based were summarized in a paper published in advance of our full report on the research (Johnson and Ransom, 1980).

> Our home interviews were with parents whose children had already been at secondary school for from one to six years. Given the lapse of time, parents could not always remember which actual schools they had named in their list of preferences. However, they were less hesitant about stating what the reasons for their preferences had been. The time of transfer from primary to secondary school had been a time of real appraisal, although the focus of appraisal was not the same in all cases.
>
> Some parents had made a child-focussed choice, based on their appraisal of their child's health, ability and temperament. Others had appraised the secondary schools, so far as they were able, and made a school-focussed choice, based on such criteria as size, whether mixed or single-sex in pupil intake, their amenities, and the degree of proximity to airport flight paths.
>
> A very few parents had appraised the educational system and made a system-focussed choice. For example, some parents living outside the boroughs studied, in local authorities where secondary education had not yet been reorganised on comprehensive lines, had expressed a preference for their child to attend a comprehensive school. Another type of system-focused choice has an historical element, in that parents had

> expressed a preference for their child to attend a comprehensive school which had previously been a grammar school rather than comprehensives which had secondary modern antecedents.
>
> Most parental preferences regarding secondary schools seemed to have been based on circumstances prevailing at the time of transfer, rather than with an eye to the ensuing five or seven years. Details of family organisation and convenience which prevailed at the time were often referred to, and any child-focussed appraisal was usually in terms of the eleven-year-old's capacity and development rather than the pupil's forthcoming adolescent years.
>
> (Johnson and Ransom, 1980, p. 182)

Two further points from our findings should be noted, as they have relevance for more recent studies of how parental choice is exercised. In the 1970s we found that in many of these working class families the choice of secondary school had been made only once, when the first and eldest child left primary school. After that, younger members of the family were expected to follow on to the same school without debate. We also found that the time when the first child left primary school was, for most families, the first time that they had dealings with the local education authority. In the two boroughs studied, the children were usually allocated to secondary schools on the basis of nearness to the home, and the presence of brothers and sisters on the roll of the school. In most cases this was acceptable to parents, who did not want their eleven-year-old sons and daughters to have to travel far, and who found it convenient to have all their children attend the same secondary school. However,

> for those parents who had attempted to make a knowledgeable choice based on other criteria (for example, those parents who had visited a number of schools to examine the facilities and in some cases question the head teacher), considerable bitterness against the education office was engendered if their preferences were not granted. The idea of parental choice was felt by such parents to be a mockery. Strong feelings were expressed, and sharp exchanges with education officers recalled, even several years after the event, when the child in question might be nearing the end of his secondary school life. *Promotion of the idea of parental choice of secondary schools may be politically counter-productive, unless the administrative reality of choice is congruent with the range of parental aspirations* (italics added).
>
> (Johnson and Ransom, 1980, p. 183)

Research in the 1980s

As we have seen, the idea of parental choice *was* formally promoted by the 1980 Education Act. Three major pieces of research were undertaken soon after, to study both the exercise of choice by parents, and the administrative reality of that choice. These enquiries will be referred to here as the 'Edinburgh', the 'Glasgow' and the 'NFER' studies.[8]

The two Scottish enquiries into parental choice naturally addressed the situation as experienced north of the border, where both central and local government of education differ from that in England and Wales.[9] Nevertheless these two research enquiries are immensely useful to all students of the policy and practice of parental choice. They demonstrate all the administrative and political quandaries connected with the operation of schemes for parental choice, as well as the conceptual and reporting difficulties which are encountered when attempting to enquire into and generalise about family behaviour.

THE EDINBURGH STUDY OF PARENTAL CHOICE

The Edinburgh study was the most ambitious in its approach to the subject. At the time of writing, the book which draws together all its findings is not yet available (Adler, Petch and Tweedie, 1989), but a wealth of journal articles and papers show the broad coverage of the research (Adler and Tweedie, 1986; Tweedie, Adler and Petch, 1986; Tweedie, 1986, 1986a; Petch 1986, 1986a, 1987, 1988; Raab and Adler, 1987; Adler, Petch and Tweedie, 1987, 1987a; Adler and Raab, 1988). The research had five aims, which were pursued as five interlinked projects:

- to examine the origins and parliamentary consideration of parental choice legislation in Britain
- to study the implementation of the legislation in Scotland
- to survey the exercise of school choice by parents
- to study the operation of appeal procedures
- to establish what the patterns of movement are between schools generated by parental choice activity

Social research is never entirely detached and Olympian in its viewpoint. Particular researchers are interested in particular things. The central focus of enquiry, for this research team, was the dilemma posed by the exercise of individual choice within a national system of education. They were concerned to view the individual parent's rights in the context of all parents' rights, and to keep in mind the authority's duty to provide education for all school-age children. The needs and aspirations of parents for their children, at both the primary and secondary stages of education, were carefully examined, but the overall conclusion of the research seemed to be[10] that the operation of parental choice was counter-productive for public education as a whole. The tendency which the researchers observed to polarize 'popular' and 'unpopular' schools would, they believed, prejudice equality of educational opportunity and render more difficult the duty placed on education authorities to provide adequate and efficient education for all. Their conclusions reinforce the 'planning' argument outlined in chapter 1.

The study began by examining significant stages in the development of parental choice legislation. Adler, Petch and Tweedie (1987) contend that in England and Wales the ideas underlying the promotion of parental choice underwent a number of changes during the 1970s. So far as the Conservative party were concerned, whereas their rationale for parental choice

> had initially emphasised freedom from state control and the assumption of parental responsibilities for their children, it was now presented as a means of improving educational standards – the introduction of market forces would force unpopular (poor) schools to close and enable popular (good) schools to expand. It was also seen to appeal to those parents whose children would previously have gone to grammar schools and who were disenchanted with comprehensive schooling, and to those who were alarmed at the growth of radical educational ideas and would welcome an attempt to cut the teaching profession down to size.
>
> (Adler *et al.*, 1987, p. 296)

It is clear from the tone of this retrospective analysis that in the 1980s at least the issues perceived to be at stake consequent upon parental choice are different from those of the expansionist Plowden era. No longer is it ingenuously assumed that LEAs will seek to 'improve' unpopular schools. Rather, the possibility of parental choice is perceived by some as a threat to the teaching profession and to certain developments in education.

The parliamentary initiatives by the Conservative party in the 1970s, to which Adler *et al.* refer, were unsuccessful. There followed an attempt by the Labour government to 'propose some parental choice legislation of its own. Eventually . . . the Labour government included a number of parental choice provisions in its 1978 Education Bill' (Adler *et al.*, 1987, p. 296). However, the Bill died in Committee when the 1979 election was called.

The authors point out that during the 1960s and 1970s there were no comparable attempts at parental choice legislation in Scotland. There was, they claim, less public concern in Scotland about educational standards or about the introduction of comprehensive schooling, and 'less support for an attack on collectivism in practice or the espousal of an individualistic ethic' (Adler *et al.*, 1987, p. 297). The idea of a parents' charter was an 'English policy, which did not easily take root in Scotland'. Nevertheless, when the 1980 Education Act introduced parental choice of school for England and Wales (see chapter 2) it was followed in due course by the Education (Scotland) Act 1981. Both the English and the Scottish Acts gave parents the right to request a place at a particular school for their child:

> education authorities are required to comply with parental requests unless a statutory exception to this general duty applies; dissatisfied parents have the right to appeal to a statutory appeal committee and, if the latter finds in favour of the parent, its decision is binding on the authority; and education authorities are required to provide parents with information about the school to which their child has been allocated and about any other school if the parents ask for it.
>
> (Adler *et al.*, 1987, p. 303)

There are however certain important differences between the two pieces of legislation. Adler *et al.*, taking the view that ideas about parental choice are not indigenous to Scotland, find it ironic that the Scottish legislation appears to establish stronger rights for parents.

> The statutory exceptions to the authorities' duty to comply with parents' requests are broad and general in England but much more specific in Scotland. In England, the primary exception, which applies when compliance with the parents' request would "prejudice the provision of efficient education or the efficient use

> of resources", *enables the authority to justify a refusal by referring to conditions at schools other than the one requested by the parents or to conditions in their schools generally*. By contrast, in Scotland, where the primary exceptions apply when compliance would entail the employment of an additional teacher or significant extensions or alterations to the school or "be likely to be seriously detrimental to order and discipline at the school or the educational well-being of the pupils there", *the authority can only refer to conditions at the school requested by the parents*. Second, parents in Scotland can appeal an adverse decision of an appeal committee to the sheriff [Education (Scotland) Act, 1981, s. 30] while parents in England have no further right of appeal. Thirdly, where an appeal committee or a sheriff upholds an appeal in Scotland, the authority must review the cases of all parents in similar circumstances who did not appeal and, if its decisions are unchanged, it must grant the parents a further right of appeal [Education (Scotland) Act, 1981, ss 28E(5) and 28F(6)]. There is no comparable provision in the English legislation (italics added).
>
> (Adler *et al.*, 1987, p. 304)

To explore how the Scottish legislation on parental choice worked out in practice, Adler and his colleagues undertook fieldwork in the three regions of Lothian, Fife and Tayside. Pupil places in Scottish schools were more uniformly allocated on the basis of catchment areas than was the case in England. Accordingly, following the 1981 Act Scottish parents had the opportunity to make a placing request for a school other than the district (or 'catchment area') school. If they did not do so, the child would automatically be allocated to the district school.

By studying the actual incidence of placing requests, the researchers found that numbers of these doubled during the period under study (1982–5 inclusive) although the overall percentage of the pupil population in respect of whom placing requests were made remained fairly low. In 1985 '9.6 per cent of pupils entering the first year of primary school and 8.7 per cent of pupils entering the first year of secondary school' were the subject of placing requests (Raab and Adler, 1987, p. 161). However these national figures mark considerable regional and local variations. The percentage of placing requests varied from less than 1 per cent in rural authorities with scattered schools to 14 per cent in Tayside. Within regions, placing requests were highest in the cities and lowest in the rural areas surrounding them. 'In 1984, 21.1 per cent of pupils entering the first year of primary school and 19.8 per cent of pupils entering the first year of secondary school in Dundee had made placing requests, compared with rates of 15.4 and 13.1 per cent for Tayside region' (Raab and Adler, 1987, p. 162). Equivalent figures in the city of Edinburgh were 16.1 per cent (primary) and 16.9 per cent (secondary), compared with rates of 11.0 and 11.8 per cent in Lothian region as a whole.

Focusing on placing requests in Edinburgh and Dundee, the researchers observe that there has been considerable movement between primary schools right across both cities and, as a result, some primary rolls have altered substantially, albeit not as much as some secondary school rolls. They take the view that so far as secondary education is concerned the legislation is producing a two tier system of desirable and undesirable schools. Two aspects of the situation appear however to be neglected in this analysis. First, the decline in the overall pupil population is undoubtedly a compounding factor in the diminution of some pupil rolls. Secondly, by focusing exclusively on the outcomes of choice in terms of size of school rolls, the authors neglect the question of whether parental satisfaction in the exercise of choice outweighs the difficulties for the authority.

Research into appeals

Not all placing requests are successful, and the study of appeal procedures was an important aspect of the Edinburgh team's research. In their view 'the extent to which adverse decisions are appealed, and the outcome of these appeals, is central to an understanding of the impact of the parental choice legislation' (Adler, Petch and Tweedie, 1987a). Their main finding about appeal committees is that they function as an extension to authorities' admission procedures, and fall in with the 'line' taken in the authority, so do not provide the effective check on the authority which the legislation intended.

The researchers point out that the primary purpose of the 1981 (Scotland) Act – like the 1980 Education Act in England and Wales – was to restrict education authorities' ability to refuse parents' school choice. 'The possibility of an appeal helps to assure that parents' rights of school choice are respected by education authorities' (Tweedie, Adler and Petch, 1986). Admission limits were placed on schools by the authority before any individual placing requests were made. When parents requested a place for their child at an oversubscribed school, the authority's justification for refusing the request rested on its judgement that the school's admission limit had been set at the correct level. Exceeding the limit by admitting more children to the school would lead to situations which the 1981 Act allowed as grounds for refusal: the need to employ an additional teacher; significant alterations to the school; detriment to order, discipline and the well-being of pupils at the school. If parents appealed against a refusal of placement, the authority had to offer evidence to justify the admission limit. If this evidence was found satisfactory by the appeal committee or sheriff, it was still their duty to determine whether refusing the request was appropriate in the particular circumstances of the appeal. The intended function of appeals was, then, to identify cases that merited special treatment in ways not recognized in the authority's policies.

Having made a detailed study of appeal procedures in two authorities, the Edinburgh researchers concluded that authorities had not yet come to an understanding of the real function of appeals. They looked on appeals as an extension of their own admission policies, rather than as an external check on their admission decisions. In one authority, the policy was for school councils[11] to interview parents in an effort to identify exceptional circumstances, and exceptions were made to the admission limit in many cases. Appeal committees served as a further extension of that general policy. The other authority aimed for the rapid processing of placing requests within schools' admission limits. Their appeal committees concentrated on enforcing the schools' admission limits, and showed little interest in special circumstances. Whether the authorities' admission limits were in fact justified under the terms of the 1981 Act did not seem to be called into question by appeal committees in either authority. In fact, questions about admission limits appeared irrelevant to their decisions.

The unpublished paper (Tweedie *et al.*, 1986) from which these conclusions are drawn contains a valuable near-verbatim account of actual appeal committee meetings observed by Tweedie. His account clearly illustrates how official bodies sometimes 'take against' articulate and insistent parents, whom they define as 'pushy'. It also demonstrates that, for parents, officers of the authority and members of the appeal committee may be indistinguishable from one another. We shall return to these points in later discussion.

If appeals against placement are not upheld at the committee stage there remains (for Scottish parents) appeal to the sheriff.[12] Here the researchers found considerable inconsistency of outcome. They conclude that two basic types of decision are being made: the 'school-level' decision which looks at the effects of additional placement on the school concerned, and the 'single-child' decision, which considers each application for placement in isolation from all others.

The research showed that when a school-level approach was followed conditions at the school were taken into account, also the fact that other parents' requests had been turned down. On the other hand, any sheriff who took a single-child approach was likely to uphold most well-presented appeals by parents. The researchers contend that authorities take their cue from the sheriff once his position is clear. In Strathclyde region, for example, where the single-child approach appears to have prevailed, most appeals are conceded by the region as soon as they are lodged with the sheriff. The Edinburgh research team are strongly opposed to the single-child approach. They point out that the relevant sections of the 1981 Act 'shift control over school admissions strongly towards parents, but they do not give parents an unconditional choice of school. They should be interpreted to give effect to the exceptions that Parliament set out: thus sheriffs using the single-child approach should abandon it and all sheriffs (and appeal committees) should adopt the school-level approach' (Adler and Tweedie, 1986, p. 308).

One further effect of the parental choice legislation which the Edinburgh study addresses is its effect on requests for under-age admission to maintained schooling (Petch, 1987). In Scotland, children normally start school between the ages of four and a half and five and a half. However, the realization that the right to make a placing request may include the right to place children in school at an earlier age than heretofore (*Boyne and Boyne v. Grampian Regional Council*, 1983) has been seized on by some parents. Placing requests and appeal procedures concerned with under-age admission substantially increased in Scotland between 1982 and 1985, and have given rise to a number of legal wrangles. Parents in England do not yet appear to have followed those of Scotland in putting pressure on authorities to concede early age admission as a valid aspect of parental choice in LEA-maintained schools. It remains to be seen whether grant-maintained schools, introduced by the Education Reform Act 1988, will, like the independent schools, prove more flexible than LEA-run schools about the age of first admission to school. If so, parents may want LEAs to adopt a similarly flexible policy.

Research with parents
All the aspects of the Edinburgh study so far discussed have related to the impact of the parental choice legislation on authorities and schools. We come now to the question of what the legislation means for parents.

One of the five aims of the research team was to study the way parents choose schools. Petch, a member of the Edinburgh team, organized a survey of 1,000 parents. About 600 of these had children who were about to start secondary school, and in the rest of the families the children were approaching primary entry. All the home interviews, conducted by a survey organization, followed a standard schedule of questions. Geographically the sample included, at both primary and secondary levels, examples of a city, a town (burgh) and a new town environment. Particular schools were targeted in each area. For example, at primary level, in the city sample, a cluster of eight adjacent schools was selected. 'For each target school, . . . the aim was to survey a sufficient number of "stayers", those not making a placing request, and an enhanced number of "requesters", those making placing requests, both in and out of the chosen schools' (Petch, 1986, p. 28).

The findings of the survey are separately presented for the primary and secondary school stages of choice (Petch, 1986 and 1986a respectively). They apply only to maintained schools, as the small number of parents choosing private schools were excluded from Petch's discussion. Overall her findings show that at both stages parental choice of school is most strongly influenced by pragmatic and pastoral considerations, 'factors which direct little attention, if any, to the actual structure of what the child will receive by way of educational content or method at the selected school' (Petch, 1986a, p. 35). At primary level choice appears to be chiefly structured by considerations of the child's happiness, safety in travelling ('the school is safer to get to'), sibling attendance at the school and its proximity to the home. At secondary level, the equivalent factors were the happiness of the child, the child's preference for the school and the 'better discipline' of the chosen school. (Reasons for rejecting the district secondary school were the exact converse of these: the child would be unhappy; the child did not want to go to the school; the school had poor discipline).

These findings lead Petch to conclude that 'at least within the state system the majority of parents who are exercising choice on behalf of their child are doing so from a humanistic rather than technological perspective, being less concerned with measurable criteria of product than with the creation of an atmosphere supportive to the child's well-being. . . It cannot be denied that the reality of behaviour appears to be very different from the parent searching for academic achievement which is commonly portrayed' (Petch, 1986a, p. 35). This cautiously worded conclusion appears to echo Elliott's (1981a) finding that process rather than product (or outcome) criteria are more important to parents choosing schools.

In making any research approach to parents enquirers are faced, as Petch (1986) points out, with the 'complex methodological problems of how most effectively to capture and interpret . . . subjective accounts'. Petch recognizes the challenge which unexpected findings present to the structured questionnaire interview: 'in a sense we can only construct such an instrument if we already know the answers'. Given the outcome of her survey she would like to delve further into what exactly parents mean by 'happiness'. Does this 'catchall' phrase perhaps embrace the idea that getting on well academically is all part of happiness at school? And if the choice of school for a child follows an earlier decision made for an older sibling, or because friends have been pupils there (as Johnson and Ransom (1983) also found), what were the reasons underlying these past decisions? Petch acknowledges that for parents to develop their explanations in greater depth, less structured interviewing would be needed (Petch, 1986, p. 46).

Turning now to the other major piece of Scottish research on parental choice, the 'Glasgow' study, we find that here an attempt has been made to explore more fully the parental point of view on opportunities for choice.

THE GLASGOW STUDY OF PARENTAL CHOICE

Macbeth, Strachan and Macaulay at the Department of Education, Glasgow University, carried out the parental choice research with funding from the Scottish Education Department, from 1982 to 1985. Their research brief was similar to that for the Edinburgh study: to monitor the implementation of sections 1 and 2 of the Education (Scotland) Act 1981, and associated regulations. Unlike the Edinburgh team, however, the Glasgow team directed almost all their research resources towards examining the effect of the parental choice legislation on families and schools.[13] Their main research tool was a questionnaire survey of 1,500 parents, supplemented by some 200 home interviews.

The researchers took the view that all parents whose child entered a Scottish school in the early 1980s were to some extent making a positive choice. Either they were 'making a placing request' in the terms of the 1981 Act or they were 'opting for the local school'. These two groups of parents were designated in the report as 'Placing Request' (PR) parents or 'No Placing Request' (NPR) parents. Both the questionnaire survey and the interviews sought information from both sets of parents, in six different areas within three Scottish regions. In addition, 140 headteachers of schools in these areas were interviewed.

The Glasgow study of parental choice is one of the largest direct research approaches to parents made in recent years, and it collected a mass of valuable material. The 339 pages of the project's 'public report' (University of Glasgow, 1986), supplemented by a further 90 pages of appendices, provides the reader with a plethora of information and discussion, summarized in 39 paragraphs of conclusions. Most of the work, however, is presented in separate case study form and it is left to the reader to make the connections between the six study areas where the work was carried out. Much can nevertheless be gleaned about parental choice from the six case studies of the Glasgow research.

The questionnaire survey

The purpose of the questionnaire[14] was to find out what parents knew of the right of choice, how they had exercised choice, what was the basis of their choice and its outcome in terms of travel to school for their child, and whether they thought parental choice important. Use of appeal procedures and their outcome was also asked about, where appropriate. The survey showed that even among NPR respondents over eighty per cent knew of their right to make a placing request (University of Glasgow, 1986, p. 335, conclusion 18). Their knowledge derived both from formal sources (school or education authority) and informal sources (media and friends).

Where reasons for choice are asked about in an open-ended way, as part of a large-scale study, obvious problems of categorization arise. For example, in one of the study areas (the urban area) 549 families advanced no less than 999 reasons for choice of school. In all six areas, reasons given were broadly categorized by the research team as school based reasons, non-school reasons and other reasons. The latter category included 'not only miscellaneous and uncategorizable reasons, but also those which might be both school based and non-school reasons at the same time' (University of Glasgow, 1986, p. 124). Since, as already noted, survey results in each of the six study areas are separately presented and discussed in the report it is not easy to form a general impression of the distribution of stated reasons among the three categories. Table 3.1 draws these together from six chapters of the report.

In the conclusions to the study Macbeth and his colleagues summarize these data as showing that 'parents' reasons for choosing a school were divided fairly equally between those which were based on assessments of schools and those which were non-school reasons'. However it should be noted that more than one reason could be cited, and almost half the parents took advantage of this. It is possible that the many parents who gave two reasons may have seen fit to include one reason about the school and another about the child or about family convenience. Without sight of the returned questionnaires the *combination* of reasons given by particular families cannot be established.

From a study of the 'reasons' tables in each of six chapters it can be noted that the 'other reasons' category in each case includes 'sibling already at the school', and this reason accounts in each area for the majority of the 'other' reasons.

It is understandable that the research team found difficulty in classifying this reason either as 'school based' or 'non-school', but the proportion of references to sibling attendance seems worthy of greater prominence than they give it.[15] It could throw further light

Table 3.1 Categories of reasons given for choosing schools, by respondents to the Glasgow Parental Choice questionnaire (expressed as percentages)

Area	School based	Non-school	Other
Urban	43.7	43.5	12.7
Suburban	48.1	37.8	14.1
Large burgh	39.7	49.8	10.6
Small burgh	28.0	61.4	10.6
Rural	40.7	47.2	12.2
Special*	55.3	36.4	8.4
Overall average	42.6	45.5	11.4

* This area of special study comprised two urban secondary schools with exceptional placing request movements, and their associated primary schools.

Note: Small differences between the category totals given in this table and Table 3.2 are due to rounding.

Source: University of Glasgow, 1986, chs 6–11.

Table 3.2 Sub-division of 'Other' reasons for choice of school given by respondents to the Glasgow Parental Choice questionnaire (as percentage of all reasons)

Area	Sibling at school	Other	Total other
Urban	10.3	2.4	12.7
Suburban	8.61	5.46	14.07
Large burgh	7.63	2.95	10.58
Small burgh	6.06	4.54	10.60
Rural	9.75	2.43	12.18
Special	6.06	2.29	8.35
Overall average	8.06	3.34	11.41

Note: Small differences between the category totals given in this table and Table 3.1 are due to rounding.

Source: Tables giving numbers of reasons for choice of school, University of Glasgow, 1986, chs 6–11.

on the extent to which parents in effect make only one choice of school, for their eldest child (as attested by some other studies). It would be desirable to know whether those parents who referred to sibling attendance were respondents who gave only one reason for their choice of school or whether other factors also influenced their decision.

However, such detail as does emerge in the report enables the conclusion that in giving school based reasons for choice (which was more common among PR than NPR parents) PR parents advanced more detailed reasons about specific facets of schooling. NPR parents actually outnumbered PR parents in their mention of vague generalizations about the quality of schools as a reason for choice ('good reputation' for example). Curricular reasons represented a minority (11%) of school based reasons. More than half of non-school reasons were related to convenience. NPR parents mentioned these more often than PR parents. Generally convenience was a more prevalent reason at primary than at secondary level (University of Glasgow, 1986, ch. 12).

Interviews with parents

The report by the Glasgow team is based not only on the questionnaire survey, but also on interviews with 200 parents, spread over the six case study locations. These were carried out by five specially recruited interviewers, who reported back to the research team.

Interview material is very different in character from questionnaire data, and it is never easy to present the two kinds of information as a coherent whole. The points which parents think it important to make to interviewers sometimes tend to decrease researchers' confidence in the more 'cut-and-dried' questionnaire replies. Has the questionnaire failed to uncover an important facet of parental choice simply because the appropriate question was not included in it? This is the dilemma already referred to by Petch of the Edinburgh team, that one needs to know what the answers will be before posing the questions. In the Glasgow study it is clear, for example, that the questionnaire did no more than scratch the surface of the family connections which are part of the background to choice of school. In one of the case study areas:

> only eight questionnaire responses, less than 12%, reported that a sibling attending or having attended a school had a bearing on the choice of that school. Yet more than half of the parents interviewed have or have had an older sibling at the chosen school, local or otherwise. These parents indicated a general level of satisfaction with the education other older children had received and saw no reason, therefore, to make a different decision for a younger child. . . . Five interviews revealed that the parent's personal experience of the school had been an influential factor, in each case to opt for the school. Three fathers were former pupils of the school chosen, in one case making a placing request for his daughter to attend that school. One interviewed mother had previously taught in the local school, and another mother was a cleaner in the local school.
>
> (University of Glasgow, 1986, p. 224)

Similarly, in another area:

> about one-sixth of parents who did not make a placing request stated in their questionnaire response that a sibling presently attending or previously having attended the school affected their choice of school for their younger child. The equivalent proportion for those who made placing requests was only one in eleven. However, over one-third of the interviewed parents indicated that siblings had been a factor taken into account. Some parents specifically stated that they wanted all their children to attend the same school, and convenience presumably was at least part of the reason for that. Others had used their experience with

> an older child to assess the school. One mother . . . would definitely have sent her child to another school if an older child had not got on so well at the local school . . . Three mothers had themselves attended the school chosen for their child, and one of these knows the headteacher and teachers of the school personally. One mother is a cleaner at the local school and often talks informally to the teachers.
>
> (University of Glasgow, 1986, p. 195)

These quotations are extracted from the report because they throw further light on the point about sibling attendance which has already been made. But the quotations also serve to illustrate the wealth of detail which a research study such as this produces, and from which it is necessary to move back before helpful conclusions can be drawn. The report contains much on which to reflect. But research cannot be deemed complete until the researchers themselves, with the benefit of their full experience, impart to the reader how their own thinking on the subject has been influenced by the research.[16]

That said, one may nevertheless wish to agree with one of the headteachers interviewed for the Glasgow study, who remarked that the *concept* of parental choice is 'desperately simplified' (University of Glasgow, 1986, p. 292). The *practice* of parental choice, on the other hand, is exceedingly complex – a point we shall return to in chapter 5.

THE NFER STUDY OF PARENTAL CHOICE

This, the third of the major studies of parental choice to be examined here, was carried out in England and Wales. As with the Edinburgh study, the central issue for the researchers was 'where the balance should lie between parental choice and LEA management' (Stillman, 1986, p. 1). A questionnaire survey was used to establish the attitude and practice of LEAs regarding parental choice following the 1980 Education Act. How were they using the 'efficient use of resources' clause in the Act, which gave the possibility of setting aside parental preference in favour of efficient administration?

LEA policies

The research showed that of the 125 authorities and divisions surveyed, 76 followed a catchment area policy. For the purpose of the study, a catchment area system was defined as one in which 'most parents were initially offered a place at just one local school' (Maychell, 1986, p. 14). In continuing to use such a policy following the 1980 Act, these authorities were presumably of the opinion that catchment areas were a prerequisite of 'efficient use of resources'. Their detailed reasons for using catchment areas (apart from the problem of travel in rural situations) were mainly:

- to protect unpopular schools by balancing numbers between catchment areas
- to promote community-based education
- to link junior and secondary schools
- to facilitate administration and the accurate forecasting of numbers

Maychell, a member of the research team, points out that although the use of catchment areas was not in itself necessarily detrimental to parental choice, the reasons local authorities gave for continuing to organize school place allocation in this way clearly indicated the 'priority afforded to other policy and practices at the expense of parental choice' (Maychell, 1986, p. 14). Moreover, the manner in which the 'reserved place' at the catchment area school was offered, and the implicit disincentives to parents to express an alternative preference, all served to minimize the exercise of choice. But in so-called 'free choice' authorities, just as in catchment system authorities, LEAs had their own ways of constraining parental choice, for example the timetabling of admission procedures with narrow deadlines for parental response; the LEA's policy with regard to transporting pupils (a vital consideration in rural areas) and the LEA's rigidity with regard to 'intended intakes' for individual schools (Stillman and Maychell, 1986).

Information for parents

The NFER research included a detailed study of the information which LEAs made available to parents, as required by the 1980 Act. Like other investigators of this topic (Muskett, 1986) the NFER team found that the legislation had generated a patchy response. 'A number of LEAs failed to meet the legal minimum, and others presented some of their information sufficiently ambiguously for it to diminish the parents' access to the system. In catchment-area authorities, the distribution of information tended to be highly localized, and individualism frowned upon. In free-choice areas we still saw many attempts to present a uniform view of schools' (Maychell, 1986, p. 19).

The LEAs' general information booklets could be misleading on two counts: the way in which they described the policy followed in deciding admission to schools, and their explanation of the statutory appeals procedure. Admissions policy, Maychell points out, was normally taken to include the admissions criteria which LEAs apply. 'There was great variation in the detail in which the criteria were described: some brochures went to considerable lengths to give precise wording and listed up to ten criteria, whilst others failed to draw attention to the criteria by phrasing the information in the text and by using broad generalisations. One authority said that it kept the criteria deliberately vague so that the parents could not engineer the system' (Maychell, 1986, p. 18).

So far as the statutory appeals system was concerned, most booklets set this out clearly, but in some cases the information about the statutory appeals system was blended with the account of the authority's admissions procedure and its non-statutory internal appeals or 'reviews' (Maychell, 1986, p. 18). The research approach to parents (further discussed below) showed that although most parents were aware they could appeal against the allocation of a school place, not all distinguished clearly between the formal appeal procedure and the informal reviews with education officers which usually took place before appeals went forward (Stillman and Maychell, 1986). As the Edinburgh study also found, parents were not always sure exactly who they were dealing with, and what their own rights were at the particular stage of the appeal.

Research with parents

To obtain parents' experience of parental choice following the 1980 Act the NFER research team issued questionnaires to over 3,000 families whose children had transferred or were about to transfer to secondary school in one of four authorities. In two of the authorities (Seatown and Northtown)[17] selective secondary education, regulated by the 11 plus examination, prevailed. A third authority, Shiretown, was fully comprehensive while in Southborough, the fourth authority studied, there was selection at the secondary stage for girls only (to two voluntary aided schools).

The parents' questionnaire, which had been developed during a two-stage pilot study, was distributed and collected through schools already taking part in the research, and achieved an 82 per cent response rate. Its main purpose was to identify the factors which influence parental decisions when children transfer to secondary school. The limited nature of the enquiry (dealing only with choice at the secondary stage of education), the high response to the questionnaire[18] and the knowledge of the schools and LEAs concerned which the researchers had already acquired, enabled them to present a thorough analysis of their research findings (Stillman and Maychell, 1986, chs 5 and 6), in which considerable confidence can be placed.

The NFER research revealed notable differences in the sense of choice of secondary school experienced by families in the four authorities and indeed by families clustered around particular groups of schools within those authorities. This sense of choice influenced families' attitudes to schools. It seemed that the more choice parents felt they had, the more time and effort they put into making their choice. Where families perceived *no* choice, neither parents nor child expressed strong feelings about the school to which the child did in fact transfer. Choice, the researchers conclude, can be an important motivating factor for family commitment to the school.

No blanket statement could be made about what factors created the *sense* of choice. The presence of voluntary schools added to perceived choice, but even when the only apparent choice was between like schools, this choice was perceived as 'real'. Here, proximity was the criterion, and if families were free to choose the school within more convenient reach, this was appreciated. Selective secondary education did not always have the same effect on families' sense of choice. In some circumstances people in 11 plus areas felt they had *no* choice, it was 'pass or fail'. In other cases, the very existence of both grammar and comprehensive schools in an area seemed to have enhanced a sense of choice for some parents, even if this choice was dependent on 11 plus outcomes.

The questionnaire asked parents to list up to five points which were important to them when choosing a school. It is of interest to note that nearly one-fifth of the parents returning the questionnaire gave no response to this question. For some parents it is no doubt difficult to separate out the many factors which influence their choice. However, '2245 parents responded to give 7689 classifiable reasons between them, an average of 3.4 reasons per responding family' (Stillman and Maychell, 1986, p. 88). Faced with this multitude of reasons, which they first classified into 97 groups, the researchers followed Elliott's (1981a) 'process or product' form of analysis. Process reasons related to how the school worked, for example its banding system or discipline. Product reasons looked to the end product of schooling, for example examination successes and university entrance rates. To this they added the category 'geography, i.e. distance from home to school . . . since it appeared to form the basis of a separate yet homogenous group' (Stillman and Maychell, 1986, p. 88).

The three-way classification of product, process or geography dealt with 80 of the NFER's 97 groups, 17 remaining unclassifiable under these headings. Most of these unclassifiable groups comprised child and family reasons (child's friends will be going there; siblings already there, and so on) or references to recommending agents such as other parents. In contrast to the Scottish studies already discussed, only a small percentage of parents, in no case more than 7 per cent, listed this type of reason. The most frequently recorded reason was a 'product' one: good standards of education, exam results or academic record were listed by 52 per cent of parents as important to their choice of secondary school. In second place came the 'process' reason of good discipline (38 per cent) (Stillman and Maychell, 1986, appendix, table 5.1). However the researchers lay stress on the *combination* of reasons given by each family. About 90 per cent of parents included process reasons in what they considered important in choosing a school. Very few parents gave product-only, or product-and-geography-only reasons, and only just over half the parents (54 per cent) gave any product reasons at all. Looked at in this way, process reasons were paramount (Stillman and Maychell, 1986, pp. 89/90).

Aspects which were important to parents when choosing a school varied according to which school their child was attending. But the *sense* of available choice could also be linked with parents' analysis of what was important to them. The more choice parents perceived they had, the more highly they rated academic record and the more widely spread were the aspects they listed (Stillman and Maychell, 1986, p. 128).

For the keen student of the many factors influencing parental choice of school, Stillman and Maychell's case studies of parents and schools in the context of four authorities are well worth reading. The authors feel they are left with two unanswered questions:

> first, how schools create a sense of commitment and belonging where pupils and parents feel they have had no choice whatever,

and secondly, whether the choice between like schools is as likely to enhance parents' feelings of a real choice and hence commitment to a school as might a choice between diverse schools.

(Stillman and Maychell, 1986, p. 155)

Conclusion

The three enquiries into parental choice on which this chapter has mainly focused all followed the 1980 Education Act (and the equivalent 1981 Act in Scotland) but preceded the 1988 Education Reform Act. They provide empirical evidence relevant to the various arguments for and against parental choice which we considered in chapter 1. The NFER and Edinburgh enquiries into how authorities attempted to manage and to some extent constrain parental choice of school are relevant for the 'planning' objection to parental choice. 'Parents' rights' are the implicit focus of research into the administration of choice procedures, and the exercise of various forms of appeal (NFER and Edinburgh). All three studies (NFER, Glasgow and Edinburgh) have something to say about 'parents as experts on their own children', and 'knowledgeable consumers in the education market'. Research has also shown the potential for conflict between these aspects of choice. For example, when planning considerations clash with parents' attempts to become knowledgeable consumers, bitterness results (Johnson and Ransom, 1980).

Our detailed examination of a number of research approaches to parents has shown that research into family behaviour presents significantly different problems from research into administrative practice. Families' reasons for preferring certain schools are evidently complex, and it is difficult to explore this complexity. Is it best to ask for reasons in the parents' own words, and then impose some *post hoc* form of analysis on these? Or should parents be 'prompted' by a suggested range of reasons? In either case, more than one reason will almost certainly be recorded, and to analyse the combination of reasons may be as important as to consider them singly. Then there is the problem of memory. Parents who took positive steps to request a school probably remember doing this, even if their request was not successful (six per cent of parents referred to such a request in the Plowden study; following the 1981 Act in Scotland, the Edinburgh research showed that an average of nine per cent of families made placing requests, but in some areas almost a quarter of parents might express a positive choice). Parents may not necessarily recall the full reasons for their expressed choice, however, particularly if their child has subsequently attended a different school from the one chosen. And if they did *not* make a placing request their reasons for accepting the allocated school may be even more difficult fully to uncover, even though the decision may well have been one of positive commitment.

As one headmaster in the Glasgow study implied, parental choice is a complex affair. Stillman and Maychell also comment that 'in authorities where choice is taken very seriously parents operate on . . . complex levels which as yet are not perceived by the LEA officers' (Stillman and Maychell, 1986, p. 153). Research into the exercise of choice in the maintained sector has so far done no more than scratch the surface, but does provide some pointers to likely developments as parents become yet more important actors on the educational stage, following the 1988 Education Reform Act. Chapters 5 and 6 will examine some of these implications. Now we turn to the private sector of education, to see what research has been done into parental choice of independent schools.

Chapter 4

Private education: research into choice

Research concerned with the private sector of education has, until the latter years of the twentieth century, paid little attention to parental choice. Research enquiry, initiated for the most part by the committed or those fervently opposed to private education, has either focused on the history and day-to-day life of independent schools (Honey, 1977; Rae, 1981; Leinster-Mackay, 1984; Walford, 1986), or else has traced the connections between private education and privilege in society (Board of Education 1944; Glennerster and Wilson 1970; Halsey, Heath and Ridge, 1984). Certain motivations have been taken for granted as applying to families choosing private education. At least until the end of the Second World War, the assumption was that traditions of social class divided the users of private and public education. Subsequently it began to be assumed that the long-term benefits of private schooling, by way of occupational and financial status, featured prominently in the minds of parents who paid for their children's education (Glennerster and Pryke, 1964). The findings of the Public Schools Commission in 1968 about the educational origins of a range of holders of high office served to strengthen this belief (Public Schools Commission, 1968, vol. ii, app. 8).

One of the few direct enquiries into parents' choice of private education was carried out by Lambert in the 1960s as part of a much wider study of boarding education. By definition he only interviewed parents who had chosen boarding schools for their children, whether in the private or the public sector (Lambert, 1975).

More recently, developments in education generally have encouraged a wider consideration of the relevance of the private sector for the debate about parental choice. This chapter will examine three studies from the mid-1980s. First, we consider my own study of the coexistence of private schools and state schools, and of families who use both types of school (Johnson, 1987). Secondly, the much larger-scale enquiry by Whitty, Edwards and Fitz (Edwards, Fitz and Whitty, 1989; Whitty, Fitz and Edwards, 1989) into the take-up and operation of the Assisted Places scheme will be examined. Finally we look at Fox's more focused research with the parents of public-school boys (Fox, 1984, 1985).

Parents whose choices span private schools and state schools

My research into the coexistence of public and private education was carried out from 1984 to 1986. Looking at the coexisting maintained and independent schools in the south-east of England at that time, it was evident that pupils moved from one sector to another, sometimes unpredictably. For example, where sixth-form colleges were part of the maintained education system, the number of independent school pupils who would seek a place in such a college could not be anticipated in any given year, but could make a substantial difference to the college's potential roll. Admission procedures and negotiations had to span the two sectors, involving both sets of providers of education – the LEA and the charitable trusts or private individuals who ran the independent schools.

The 16 plus stage was not the only point at which there was movement between the sectors. Of equal interest to me – and of greater relevance to my discussion here – was the repeated exercise of parental choice across the sectors, where families scanned the locally available examples of public and private education in search of what was best for their child at a particular stage. My research accordingly included work both with providers of education in both the maintained and private sectors, and with consumers of education who did not rule out either private schools or state schools when exercising parental choice (Johnson, 1987).

A primary aim of my research was to widen understanding of how parental choice is exercised in practice. I was particularly anxious that parents should not see the enquiry as in any way sponsored by the schools their children currently attended. Accordingly, I approached parents as free-floating consumers of education, through the pages of the local press.[1] I wanted to make contact with families who had already used both public and private education for their children, to explore what their motives and experience had been. I received responses from eighty-five families, and I made a detailed study of twenty-five of these.

Parents taking part in the research were from differing age groups, and material from the interviews spanned forty years of educational decision-making. All the families had, by definition, reached the 'threshold of affordability' which enabled them to consider fee-paying education for at least part of one of their children's schooling, but it was the combined income of both partners which, in the majority of cases, made this possible. Many of them were teachers. My methods, and findings as to whether private schools and state schools constituted two systems or one, are fully discussed elsewhere (Johnson, 1987). 'In-depth' research of this kind does not have predictive power or provide the basis for statistical generalizations, but it offers insights into a usually undocumented area of private family life. By spending many hours in interview with each of the twenty-five families, I was able to encourage them to tell the story of their educational decision-making for their children in their own words, and in considerable detail. These accounts were then analysed and found to illustrate particular recurring themes.

For this discussion of research into parental choice of the private sector, it is useful to note that eight themes emerged as explanations of why these families, faced with fee-paying and state education, in an area where both types of school had a good reputation, had sometimes decided to use the private schools. The following characterizations of these families reflect the themes which were defined in the course of the study:

- users and ex-users of direct grant or similar low-fee schools
- satisfied customers of the maintained grammar schools
- 'natural' users of the private sector (for whom the state system served as a temporary substitute)
- aspiring users of fee-paying education (who considered it was 'bound to be better')
- parents alienated by their contemporary experience of state primary education
- parents alienated by their contemporary experience of state secondary education
- families with boarding need
- parents looking for a school to benefit a problem child

Their experience illustrated some of the ways in which families appraise the available range of private schools and state schools. In summarizing, I tried to relate their exercise of choice either to the 'complementary' paradigm of public and private education, where the two sectors are seen as offering different educational opportunities which together provide a wide range of choice, or the 'competitive' paradigm, where private schools and state schools are seen as seeking to achieve identical aims, but with differing degrees of success. These two paradigms are highly relevant for the analysis of parental choice as it develops following the 1988 Education Reform Act, when a wider range of schools within the maintained sector (grant-maintained, city colleges, and perhaps more specialized 'magnet' schools diversifying the existing local authority schools)[2] will be coexisting with the independent schools. Will parents be choosing on a basis of competitive performance, between schools which are broadly similar in their aims, or will they perceive the enlarged range of schools as complementary, each school offering a package rather different from the others, one of which may be more suited to their child's needs?

When applied to the experience of twenty-five families who had used both public and private education, the competitive or the complementary paradigms appeared to fit some examples of parental choice, but in other cases were not fully explanatory.

For parents whose present-day decision-making was influenced by their earlier experience of direct grant schools, it could be said that what had once been a competitive situation was now perceived as complementary provision. The direct grant schools, in their heyday, were in competition with the maintained grammar schools which were then numerous in the public sector of education. Direct grant schools and grammar schools had similar aims, but for some families the direct grant schools represented a standard of excellence beyond that of the maintained grammar schools. Families with experience of maintained education who obtained a subsidized or free place for their child in a direct grant school often scarcely felt they were moving to private education. Rather, they were dealing with the 'top of the range' of available grammar schooling – a clearly 'competitive' form of provision. But once the direct grant schools were phased out, in 1975, those independent schools which were now ex-direct grant schools still represented, for some families, the same desirable standard of excellence. Now, however, they perceived the schools as having aims which were no longer shared by any broadly comparable schools in the maintained sector (since grammar schools had nearly all become comprehensive in their curriculum and intake). In that sense the two sectors had ceased to compete, and had become 'complementary'.

The twenty-five families also included parents

> who had been satisfied customers of the maintained grammar schools, either for themselves or for their children, and who now concluded that 'more of the same' was only available in the private sector. These families had either not been aware of, or had disregarded, the competition offered by direct-grant or other fee-paying grammar schools when the maintained grammar schools existed. The fee-paying schools only came into focus for these families when maintained selective secondary education was wound up.
>
> (Johnson, 1987, p. 135)

Both these themes of choice were influenced by living memory of a kind of schooling which was no longer available on the same terms (direct grant schools and maintained grammar schools which had been reorganized on comprehensive lines in the areas in question). Neither the complementary nor the competitive paradigm was wholly applicable to these families' approach to choice. Rather, it was based on an historical residue, a memory of what had been.

This analysis suggests that, as changes continue in education, other such influences may continue to affect parents' choice of schools. They may well seek, for their children, a school which appears most to resemble the school they themselves attended but which may no longer exist (for example, a voluntary comprehensive school may have become a city technology college, or an all-ability school may now be marketed as a 'magnet' school, attractive to children of particular talents or interests). A nostalgia for the 'ordinary comprehensive' of former years may become an influence on parental choice. Equally, it is possible that grant-maintained schools will take on some of the aura of the former direct grant schools, because of their closer association with central government and separation from the policies of the local authority.[3] The past will always have some influence on the present, in the exercise of parental choice.

Two further themes of movement from public to private education which I identified and which seemed fully to fit the competitive paradigm were those of 'natural' users of the private sector for whom private education was a family tradition, but who used the state system as a temporary substitute, and those who considered that fee-paying education was 'bound to be better'.

For those families to whom private education came 'naturally', it had been a positive choice to place their child in a maintained school (often a primary school) which seemed to them to offer similar or better schooling than that available in independent schools. For a while at least these families had seen the maintained and independent schools as competing providers of much the same educational experience. In the end, they moved their child to the private sector, the maintained school having after all been found wanting on this competitive basis.

As for the families who felt education which was paid for was 'bound to be better', I concluded

> these families too were using a competition model, a competition in which the private sector was, for them, in a position to win hands down. This was not because the independent schools were seen as educating a different type or class of child. Most of the parents who took the 'bound to be better' view of private education pointed out that in a suburban area the families who used private schools and state schools were indistinguishable and frequently interchanging. But the financial contract between home and school encouraged teachers to mobilise the potential of each and every child, and made the teacher–parent relationship a more equal partnership where both saw each other as legitimately in the business of seeking the child's advancement. In competing with maintained schools to educate children, the schools where fees were paid therefore drew on resources of teacher and parent commitment and motivation which were simply not present in 'free' education, in these parents' view.
> (Johnson, 1987, p. 136)

In the post-Reform-Act world of education, new opportunities may be perceived by parents to find schools where motivation of all concerned is high and parents and teachers have a common interest in getting the best out of the school. Grant-maintained status is intended to tap just such resources of autonomous commitment. It remains to be seen whether it will do so, once the novelty of transfer has settled into a new routine.

Where families had moved to the private sector because they wanted or needed boarding education for their children, this could have been a case of imperfect knowledge of the market. Those who advised them (usually their employers) appeared unaware that boarding places existed in the maintained sector. Boarding education and private education were seen as synonymous. These parents felt their choice had been structured by the complementary existence of independent (boarding) education alongside maintained sector (day) schools. In practical terms they were right, in that scarcely any boarding places were available in the maintained schools of the area.

For most of the other cases of movement from the public to the private sector of education which I analysed, the consumer's point of view did not fit fully within either the competitive or the complementary paradigm. These were families who had been alienated by their contemporary experience of particular primary or secondary schools in the public sector. In some but not all cases the children themselves were seen as part of the problem, being unsuited to the style of teaching on offer. They took the decision to move their children from maintained to independent schools.

> These parents all had clear expectations of what maintained education, whether at the primary or secondary stage, should be able to provide for their child. They did not all have the same expectations, and they recognised that other parents might not want the same thing as themselves. They therefore did not anticipate or require that each maintained school should be like any other maintained primary or secondary school. What they did hope for was to identify a school whose style and aims appeared to match their own expectations and their child's needs, to be able to get a place for their child at that school and to find that the school was managed in a way that enabled its aims to be systematically furthered. This expectation of having access to an identifiable and coherent institution was not fulfilled by their experience in maintained education in the 1980s, and they turned to private education to see if their expectations could be matched there.
>
> (Johnson, 1987, p. 136)

What these parents seemed to appreciate, as their children settled in to the chosen independent school, was that the school stated clearly what it was set up to do, and did it single-mindedly. The school had a recognizable *raison-d'etre*, which it fulfilled. And because of the fee paying factor, the exercise of choice was more in the parents' hands than with the more uncertain choice procedures of the maintained sector.[4]

Here again it seems possible that in the 1990s maintained education will be more strongly in a position to compete with independent schools for consumers who are seeking such clarity of of purpose. Current policy is encouraging all maintained schools to identify and promote their selling points, and to make their aims more clearly defined and visible to interested families. What will be the testing point is whether maintained schools 'deliver the goods' they have promised, as independent schools must usually do in order to survive.

My interviews with twenty-five families showed that these parents were extremely flexible in the criteria they applied to the choice of schools for their children. What was seen as suitable for one child in the family was not necessarily appropriate for another.[5] Although a majority of the seventy-two children in question ended up in private schools, some individuals moved from independent to state schools, and others spent all their school days in the maintained sector. These parents were as careful in their choice of local authority schools as they were of schools in the fee-paying sector, and often went to considerable lengths to get one child on to the roll of a particular maintained or aided school. Their decision-making style fully supported Coons and Sugarman's thesis that parents know their children and are best fitted to make educational choices on their behalf.

As already acknowledged, one cannot generalize from a judgement sample[6] of this kind, but there is no reason to suppose that these parents were unique in their willingness and indeed eagerness to make choices in education. Greater diversity in the maintained sector, together with more clear-cut opportunities for choice, may well wean families like these away from the costly independent schools.

The Assisted Places scheme

The families I interviewed had used their own judgement (and money) when choosing private education. The Assisted Places scheme, by contrast, represents an invitation by government to low-income families to move their children from maintained to independent schools with the help of public money. Although an assisted place can be claimed for a child already in independent education, any school which takes part in the scheme must balance its offer of assisted places on a 60/40 basis between children in maintained schools and those already being educated privately.

The Assisted Places scheme was introduced by the 1980 Education Act, and can perhaps be seen as a forerunner of things to come on the educational scene, during the successive Thatcher administrations of the 1980s. At one time it was thought that a voucher system might follow, enabling parents to choose from independent as well as maintained schools for their children, but this was not to be (Seldon, 1986). Although subsequent government initiatives have all focused on maintained schools, the Assisted Places scheme has been seen as politically and educationally significant, and an important subject for research. The Assisted Places Project, directed by Whitty and Edwards, was funded by the ESRC from 1982–1986 (Edwards, Fitz and Whitty, 1989).[7]

Like most of the research into parental choice in the maintained sector of education discussed in chapter 3, the Assisted Places Project was not solely concerned with exploring the effect of the scheme from the parents' point of view. The researchers' overall aim was to contribute to 'longstanding arguments about the academic costs associated with comprehensive education and the social costs associated with academic selection' (Whitty, Fitz and Edwards, 1989, p. 138). In studying the operation of the Assisted Places scheme during the mid-1980s they were interested to examine the relationship between claims made for the scheme by its advocates and critics, and its actual operation and effects.

The team focused their research effort on three clusters of LEAs in the south-east, north-east and north-west of England. They drew on local knowledge, augmented by information 'solicited by letter from primary heads in one of the areas' and their fieldwork with independent school pupils and parents, to develop a broad understanding of school networks in the three areas. They identified a number of local maintained schools where research parallel to that carried out in the private sector, in the form of interviews with heads, teachers, pupils and parents, would supplement understanding of the impact of the Scheme on schools and school choice in the areas (Edwards *et al.*, 1989, p. 121).

In the early days of the research the team experienced considerable difficulty in gaining access either to independent schools or maintained schools to carry out interviews. The Assisted Places scheme, whereby public money was to be spent on certain children's private education, was recognized as a controversial development in education policy. The 1980 Education Act, in referring to the 'benefit' which some pupils might derive from education at independent schools (Education Act 1980, s. 17(1)), could be seen as implicitly devaluing the education available in the public sector. Some maintained schools wanted to have nothing to do with research interested in the scheme; some independent schools, although participant in the scheme did not want attention focused on this, and in particular they did not want pupils whose education was funded by an assisted place to be singled out from normal fee-payers, in case this stigmatized them in some way (Edwards *et al.*, 1989, p. 98). In the event the research team interviewed pupils from both groups, as well as pupils in maintained grammar schools and comprehensive schools. Similar information was collected from all pupils, and this enabled a comparison to be made of the socioeconomic status and attitudes to choice of school of pupils in different educational situations. This information was verified and supplemented by home interviews with pupils' parents. In all, over 300 families were involved (Edwards *et al.*, 1989, p. 7).

In this study of take-up of the Assisted Places scheme, the social class and education background of parents participating in the scheme were seen as of prime importance. Was the scheme being used by working-class families or not? Whitty *et al.* (1989) point out that one of the major justifications for introducing the Assisted Places scheme was that it would enhance and extend the notion of parental choice. Interested parties in the independent sector involved in the pre-negotiation of the scheme before it was incorporated in the 1980 Education Act claimed that it would make it possible for able children from working-class families to benefit from an academically oriented secondary education. This opportunity, it was claimed, had existed in the days of the direct grant grammar schools, and of the award by LEAs of free places at these and certain other independent secondary schools.

The findings of the Assisted Places Project, in line with analyses of assisted place take-up prepared by the Assisted Place Unit at the DES, confirm a tendency for single-parent families, headed by women, to be the principal group taking advantage of the Assisted Places scheme. Their relevant income is low (as it has to be, to qualify for the award of an assisted place) but these families are, in the words of another writer (Douse, 1985) the 'artificially poor', that is families made so by death, divorce or unemployment. These single parents may not be well off, but yet be well endowed in terms of their own educational background, so that 'low income may be partly compensated for by the cultural capital available to the child'. The researchers found that 'other kinds of families also thought to be unduly disadvantaged' (among whom they instance parents in semi-skilled and unskilled manual work, and black and Asian families) 'are either much less prominent or conspicuously under represented' (Edwards *et al.*, 1989, p. 166). The researchers criticize the Assisted Place scheme for taking no account of the cultural and educational situation of families, nor of their assets and wealth, only their 'relevant income'. The scheme was not helping children from areas where maintained education was in difficulty. Rather, it appeared to be 'attracting middle class children who would otherwise go to good comprehensives' (Edwards *et al.*, 1989, p. 148).

From the point of view of our discussion of parental choice, part of the interest of Whitty, Fitz and Edwards' work lies in its investigation of how parents using a variety of independent and maintained secondary schools had perceived and exercised the choice available to them.

During the home interviews, parents were read out a list of factors 'sometimes said to be important in choosing a school', namely: 'location of school; social composition; facilities at school; ethos and attitudes of school; family tradition, relatives, child's friends; child's aspirations. Were these very important, somewhat important or not very important in their choice of the child's school? As a 'supplementary' to this question, parents were also asked: In terms of your own aspirations for your child, which of the following factors were particularly important for you?

- exam subjects offered
- exam results of school
- university prospects
- job and career prospects
- friendship patterns
- extra-curricular activities

Table 4.1 amalgamates the two questions and gives the percentage of cases in which parents indicated that a particular factor was 'very important'. It will be noted that social composition, child's aspirations, and exam subjects offered do not figure in this table.

Commenting on the table, the authors underline 'the widespread importance given to the academic aspects of school choice – to examination results and the ladder of opportunity to higher education and "good" jobs . . . The vague concept of "ethos" has to be included in this "academic" category because while it

Table 4.1 Selected factors determining school choice (percentage of parents naming these as very important)

	Total	Fee	AP	Comp	Gram
Examination results	51.4	58.5	54.4	40.2	72.0
Higher education	49.2	58.5	56.7	32.0	76.0
Career prospects	40.4	50.0	51.0	25.4	44.0
School facilities	41.1	43.9	46.7	36.9	32.0
School ethos	54.2	58.5	62.2	42.6	68.0
Family tradition	8.5	7.3	7.8	9.0	12.0
School location	28.2	36.2	22.2	27.9	24.0
Extra-curricular activities	24.1	32.9	20.0	21.3	24.0
Child's friends	19.4	8.5	11.1	32.8	20.0

Source: Edwards, Fitz and Whitty, 1989, Table 9.1, p. 191.

certainly included the "civilising" characteristics which had been important to some independent school parents, its essential component was a school's perceived capacity to provide a demanding and competitive setting which would "push" or "stretch" able pupils'. They also note that 'among those parents who were paying full fees, family tradition was overtly relatively unimportant. Perhaps the most striking difference . . . was the greater weight given by comprehensive school parents to where their child's friends were going' (Edwards *et al.*, 1989, p. 190).

The Assisted Places scheme only covers secondary education. This is a stage at which the pupils themselves may have developed clear preferences for particular schools or types of school. The pupil interviews which the research team conducted (in independent, grammar and comprehensive schools) were not however primarily concerned with how the choice of school was made, but with the pupils' current secondary school experience and future aspirations. All these interviews took place on school premises. The researchers found much variation in 'how socially disruptive the transition to secondary school had been, and how far it had carried the children into an initially unfamiliar social world' (Edwards *et al.*, 1989, p. 206). One marked difference between assisted place pupils' experience and the experience of other children (including fully fee-paying pupils in independent schools) was the very small extent to which 'best friends' from previous schools were still fellow-pupils. Edwards *et al.* interpret educational decision-making at the level of school choice as a 'continuously negotiated process taking place between pupils and their parents' (Edwards *et al.*, 1989, p. 214). We can perhaps conclude that the opportunity to continue earlier friendships was not a weighty point of negotiation when family decisions about assisted places were made.

Another important aspect of the Assisted Places project was its study of the way in which particular schools in either sector presented themselves to parents, and the effect on the schools themselves of the presence of academically selective schools (both maintained grammar schools and independent schools) and of the local availability of 'free', assisted or fee-paying schooling.

One of the first findings of this aspect of the study was the strength of feeling opposed to the notion of competition in education by some LEAs and heads of maintained schools. This led them on principle to be resistant to the research into assisted places, a scheme which they perceived as essentially competitive both in its ideology and its operation.

Not all those who refused access for the research did so on principle, however. Some heads refused because of current problems in the school (such as the long-running teacher action in support of a pay claim). Edwards *et al.* noted that the maintained-school heads who were most welcoming to the research, and took most personal interest in it, were those whose approach to marketing their school was closest to that of the independent sector. The research team eventually undertook research in 14 maintained primary schools, 14 secondary schools (11 of which were comprehensive) and one tertiary college, in addition to their work in 25 independent schools. Because of the problems of access, their work may under-represent the views of those maintained-school headteachers whose response to the Assisted Places scheme, and perhaps to the effect of a policy for parental choice, was to ignore it. We shall return to this point in a later chapter.

The Assisted Places Project is nevertheless invaluable in its delineation of real patterns of choice, cooperation and competition between schools in the 1980s. The researchers found considerable evidence that the opportunity for parental choice provided by the 1980 Education Act had already led to certain maintained secondary schools, notably 11–16 comprehensives, being avoided by parents. Moreover, primary heads were directing academically able pupils away from such schools.

In at least one of the areas investigated there was pressure by the LEA on the headteachers of maintained primary schools not to communicate with Assisted Place schools about applicants, nor to publicize the scheme's existence. This was partly a principled objection (because the Assisted Place scheme appeared to imply that the maintained sector was non-academic), but also because of problems with falling rolls, possible school amalgamations and intensifying difficulties with 16 plus provision. Any 'Government-sponsored exodus' from the public sector offered a further threat (Edwards *et al.*, 1989, p. 147). However, in other LEAs those running the maintained sector were seen also to have a personal interest in the success of the independent sector. The Director of Education and most of the secondary headteachers sent their daughters to the same independent girls' school (Edwards *et al.*, 1989, p. 133).

Whatever the attitude of the LEA, many primary heads continued to play a key role in identifying families who might be interested in the Assisted Places scheme, and also in by-passing those who were perceived as unsuitable. One such headteacher told the Whitty and Edwards team that poor people were not generally interested in 'that kind' of education, would not be capable of passing the examination, and for both reasons would be unlikely to figure in the scheme. The advice given by primary heads and the teachers of fourth year juniors appeared to be very influential on the type of secondary school to which the child transferred. Even in a borough where headteachers' orientations towards the scheme seemed to be negatively influenced by the political preferences of the Labour council, there was evidence that primary school teachers were encouraging particular children to take entrance examinations for independent schools (Edwards *et al.*, 1989, p. 141). In my own research (Johnson, 1987, p. 60), I found examples of primary schools where the transfer of a substantial number of school leavers to independent education was seen as a mark of success for the school they left behind.

The 'leakage' from the maintained sector at the end of the primary years was not always evident to the secondary headteachers interviewed for the Assisted Places Project. One head made special enquiries before the arrival of the research team, and learned of the 'loss' of 20 pupils from a middle school who might otherwise have joined his secondary school at its intake age of 13 years (Edwards *et al.*, 1989, p. 145). For most heads, the relevant evidence was not available. However in at least one of the areas investigated in the research, there was some traditional substantial participation in independent education by the local population. The comprehensive schools were conscious of the independent competition, but not specifically troubled by the Assisted Places scheme. Moreover the general ability level of the local cohorts of pupils meant that even with many able pupils pursuing an independent education, the maintained schools still had a substantial number of high ability children in their pupil populations. The notion of the role of a 'critical mass' of able children in keeping a school buoyant was referred to by several maintained school heads.

Even within a cluster of schools, the research team found that the belief of heads in their own school's capacity to compete with the Assisted Places scheme varied considerably, as did their degree of resignation to the notion that some members of each year cohort would inevitably be lost to the Assisted Place schools. One head was 'outraged at some of the kids who haven't come here this year' and highly critical of the primary heads who had encouraged these pupils' applications to independent schools. Another head took the strictly professional view that the client was free to make choices, and remained philosophical even when the younger son of the chairman of governors went to an independent school on an assisted place rather than joining his elder brother at the maintained school (Edwards *et al.*, 1989, p. 129).

The research team concluded that in this particular area only the well established 11–18 maintained schools with traditional sixth forms were effectively competing with the Assisted Place schools for children of the academic ability needed to gain such a place. But they found no sign that this group of high grade comprehensive schools were being stimulated by the scheme to better themselves. Nor did the heads interviewed anticipate that less favoured schools might pull themselves up in the competitive league. A 'downward spiral' was seen as more likely, and this could apply even to 'good' comprehensives. The loss of the ability range, by leakage of the most able to the independent sector, was what might 'tip the balance' for such schools, possibly coupled with loss of public confidence in the maintained sector for other reasons. Some of the problems to which heads of successful comprehensive schools referred included the effects of prolonged teacher action on parents, being the 'nut in the nutcracker' between a good local independent school and a 'Marxist' city council, and certain curriculum initiatives in maintained schools which made such schools seem overly vocational rather than academic.

In one of the areas researched, where the LEA had retained selective secondary education, certain specific factors were felt to make a difference in the relationship between maintained schools and the independent sector. Primary headteachers pointed out that, in this area, many children who might have sat independent entrance examinations did not do so. The maintained grammar schools were well regarded locally, and were put forward by estate agents as assets in the sale of local properties. Even so, the grammar schools to some extent still saw themselves as having a place in a hierarchy of local schools, with certain independent schools at the top of the league (especially where the LEA had previously awarded places to these schools as an accolade for the most able pupils).

The availability of single-sex education in the maintained sector meant that, for example, a girls' grammar school was in more direct competition with the independent girls' schools which it much resembled. Leaving aside the selectivity of its intake, this school undoubtedly benefited from being for girls only. The head reported that the school lost pupils whenever there was talk of amalgamation with a boys' school, whether or not this proposal was linked with comprehensive reorganization (Edwards *et al.*, 1989, p. 133).

The possibility of grant-maintained status for schools in the maintained sector was already in the air at the time of this research into Assisted Places. There was apprehension on the part of some in the public sector of education that opting out could be at least as great a threat as the Assisted Place scheme, since the schools most likely to opt out could rob the LEA of much of the variety it had on offer (Edwards *et al.*, 1989, p. 141).

Much of the authors' analysis deals with the response by the maintained sector to the coexistence of independent schools and the operation of the Assisted Places scheme. Slightly less is said from the point of view of the independent schools themselves about how the Assisted Place scheme affected their operations and their relations with the maintained schools. Some of the independent schools had social and sporting links with maintained grammar schools which pre-dated the Assisted Places scheme, and did not seem to have been disturbed by it. On the whole, however, there were few contacts across the sectors at the secondary level, partly due to local authority pressure on the maintained sector to keep aloof from the independent schools. Nevertheless some primary schools, as we have seen, did not break off all contact with the independent schools which were keen to take on their pupils at the secondary stage. Although some LEAs had rules forbidding the supply of information to Assisted Place schools about primary schoolchildren who were seeking such a place, these primary schools continued to cooperate with the Assisted Place schools.

In the opinion of the independent school headteachers concerned, these teachers may have been putting at risk their chances of further promotion in the maintained sector (Edwards *et al.*, 1989, p. 133).

The research team noted that in one area, a third of all the pupils in five local independent schools had Assisted Places, a proportion which reveals how severely some parts of the private sector would be affected if the scheme were to be abandoned by a future government (Edwards *et al.*, 1989, p. 147). In my own research (Johnson, 1987) I found that some independent school heads did not want to take on the 'hostages to fortune' which Assisted Place pupils represented, in that the schools concerned would be unable to support them through their whole school career if the scheme were abruptly withdrawn. However, most of the independent heads whom Edwards *et al.* interviewed appeared to be welcoming the scheme as lessening their dependence on fee-paying parents, and giving the schools the opportunity to raise the academic quality of their intake. The Assisted Place research raises the question of what effect grant-maintained schools, and other new opportunities for parental choice such as city technology colleges, will have on existing independent as well as maintained schools.

Edwards, Fitz and Whitty's research provides many insights into the effects of public money being made available to help families use the private sector of education. But it must not be overlooked that the great majority of families who choose private education for their children do so in the knowledge that they will have to pay full fees. The next research project to be discussed investigates these families.

Parents of public schoolboys

The final research study to be examined in this chapter is restricted in its scope, in that it focuses exclusively on families whose son or sons attended a boys' public school (Fox, 1984; 1985). However Fox single-handedly interviewed a relatively large number of families, and her work provides data on a hitherto unexplored aspect of parental decision-making. What is it that motivates parents to pay substantial fees for their son's education in a public school? Many observers have offered their opinion on this but the parents themselves 'have largely remained silent about their reasons for doing so' (Fox, 1984). Her focus was on the traditionally independent public schools, rather than those which had at one time been grant-aided by government. Between 1979 and 1980 she interviewed 190 sets of parents. Fox's particular interest was in whether use of private education now represented a rejection of the comprehensive secondary education widely available in the maintained schools, or whether social exclusivity or the assumed availability of a pathway to top positions were what attracted parents.

The findings of Fox's study challenged commonly held assumptions about the homogeneous social origins of all public school parents.

> Whilst it has been possible to identify amongst the sample of fathers who use today's public schools a small elite . . . 7% of the total, who exhibit a high degree of social closure in terms of both recruitment and marriage the remaining members are heterogeneous with respect to their current occupations and the degree of success within them as well as their own social origins and those of their wives. Though in these same terms the parents cannot be said to be a microcosm of society, neither can they be described as homogeneous and therefore they bring with them the potential for a wide range of attitudes, beliefs and styles of living.
>
> (Fox, 1985, p. 40)

She adds that 'with the exception of the farmers, two-thirds of the wealthy fathers who use the public schools today have created rather than acquired their wealth' (p. 49) and claims that 'the public schools today . . . incorporate into their midst . . . a minimum of 43% of boys whose parents were not themselves strictly schooled into their subculture' (p. 52). These fathers had their education not in fee-paying public schools, but in maintained grammar schools.

If such a substantial minority of parents were not themselves privately educated, is it perhaps because of the 'path to the top' that they choose public schools for their sons? Fox's respondents did not confirm this.

> The parents interviewed were reluctant to specify the types of jobs that they envisaged, let alone desired, for their sons – vehemently asserting that such ambitions are both unrealistic and futile. In a world which is seen as open to individuals to succeed and to fail according to merit and ambition it is pointless and possibly dangerous to cherish dreams whose translation into

> reality cannot be ensured. The most that the majority of parents realistically believe they can do is to offer their sons the best opportunity to make what they can of their lives, and a public school education is a part of this offering. Given the perceptions of the nature of the class structure today, fluid in the middle with an upper class which is seen either as non-existent or as closed to upward mobility, it would in turn be unrealistic to believe that many parents are using the public schools to facilitate the entry of their sons into the very top positions in society. Whilst they may wish for such a future for their sons it is much more likely that their immediate concern is to ensure that they offer them the chance to succeed in maintaining current class position in a world which is seen as increasingly competitive and where success is believed to be dependent upon the possession not only of technical skills but also of the appropriate values – ambition, deferred gratification and above all the determination to succeed.
>
> (Fox, 1984, p. 52)

As to whether choice of the private sector at the end of the 1970s was triggered by dissatisfaction with maintained and in particular comprehensive education, Fox reports that 'only a third of the parents interviewed actually expressed direct criticisms of the maintained sector'. They were not without experience of state schools. Most had friends and relatives who had recently used the schools for their children and three-quarters of them had direct contact with the maintained sector, using it for the whole or part of the education of some or all of their own children. A quarter of the parents had at least one child in a state secondary school and a further fifty per cent had made use of the primary schools, an experience which, Fox suggests, may have affected some of them in their choice of secondary schools.

> Some parents may have used the primary school as a pre-preparatory school with their children destined for the private sector regardless, whilst others have genuinely turned to the public schools only after their disappointment with what they found in the primary school.
>
> (Fox, 1984, p. 55)

The public schools chosen by Fox's respondents included both boarding and day schools. Both sets of parents mentioned most frequently the same two advantages which they believed public schools to have over the state secondary schools: 'the ability to produce better academic results and to develop the character by instilling discipline'. The discipline which Fox's parents have in mind is that of 'learning to live in a world which has rules' (Fox, 1984, p. 58).[8]

Fox believes that parents who choose public schools for their promise of 'academic success and the ability to accept discipline, necessitated by occupational success', have 'largely abdicated their collective responsibility for the maintained sector'. She concludes that 'the disappearance of the grammar schools and the continued existence of a private sector alongside a maintained sector which is organised on non-selective principles serves to polarise the experiences of those who use the two sectors of education' (Fox, 1984, p. 61).

Conclusion

For our purposes, the main interest of all these enquiries into the use of private education must be what light the studies shed on the implementation of parental choice as a broad policy. Although it may be difficult to get a place at some independent schools, parental choice is the essence of the admission procedure to schools of the private sector. Children are not 'allocated' to independent schools. The initiative rests with the parents to seek a place. So in looking at parents who have chosen private schools we are looking at people who have actually done what all parents are now presumed to want and be able to do – select a school for their child.

The three studies all appear to have made contact with what Whitty *et al.* term 'educational families' – parents who involved themselves in decisions about their children's education whether or not the proposed destination was an independent or a maintained school. Their interest and involvement may perhaps be indicative of what Baron *et al.* (1981) defined as a 'petit bourgeois' frame of mind (see chapter 1). However the social origins and (certainly in the case of my own study) the lifestyles of these families were varied, and may therefore provide some evidence that the desire to make choices in education is not confined to a particular social class. My earlier study of working class parents (Johnson and Ransom, 1983) also confirms this. Moreover, Whitty *et al.* found that the willingness to express a choice seems to increase with the scope of choice available, while parents appear more apathetic where little variety exists. This is another indication that the motivation or lack of motivation to make choices may be linked to local educational circumstances rather than social class.

What remain unresolved by the three studies, however, are the criteria which parents apply to their choice of an independent school. The families I interviewed appeared to be making highly individualized choices, focusing on the needs and interests of the particular child. For Whitty, Fitz and Edwards, and also for Fox, it seemed that academic selectivity was the key to choice of private education, and that this constituted some kind of rejection of the maintained comprehensive schools. The difference in our findings may be due to the fact that my research elicited responses from families whose experience of private education covered a wide range of preparatory and senior independent schools which varied in size, fees and objective, whereas the two studies of Assisted Place and public schools focused on independent secondary education in schools of notable academic achievement.

The other important issue on which these studies throw some light is the effect of parental choice on schools of all kinds and their relations with one another. This subject will be returned to in the next chapter.

Chapter 5

The effects of choice

Parental choice is a key element of the government's policy for education. Whether it would continue to be so, following a change of government, is a matter for future speculation, which will be briefly considered in our final chapter. But as the decade of the 1990s begins, parental choice is with us as a feature of educational decision-making. What can we say about its effects? This chapter will extrapolate from research findings about choice *prior* to the Education Reform Act, coupled with experience and observation of the educational scene *since* the Act, to reflect on the effects of choice at the level of the system, the institutions and the users. What does a policy of parental choice mean for the notion of a 'system' of education? What does it mean for the schools, and their relationships with each other? What does it mean for parents themselves, for their children, and for family attitudes to education?

Choice and the educational system

Discussion of the scope of choice (in chapter 2) has already shown that we do not have a single nation-wide system of education, but rather a network of related systems, within each of which considerable variety is to be found. The maintained sector of education, which has the greatest claim to the title of 'system' in that it is the focus of most educational legislation, is itself made up of local authority ('county') schools and voluntary schools, which may have an affiliation both to a local education authority and also a diocesan education body. Now there are also grant-maintained schools, over which the local authority has no jurisdiction, but which while receiving their funding directly from the secretary of state may purchase some continuing link to the LEA by 'buying in' to some of the authority's services. All of these sub-systems coexist with a wide variety of independent schools which may (or may not) foster professional links with one another and with maintained schools,[1] and which are subject to government inspection but not to all aspects of educational legislation.[2]

In view of all this complexity, to understand the effects of a policy of parental choice on the broad system of education, we need to give separate consideration to its effects on the role of central government, the LEAs and the diocesan education bodies.

EFFECTS AT THE CENTRE

The Reform Act as a whole has greatly strengthened the power of the centre. Maclure (1988) puts it succinctly:

> [The Reform Act] restored to the central government powers over the curriculum which had been surrendered between the Wars, and set up formal machinery for exercising and enforcing these powers and responsibilities.
>
> Not only did it strengthen the central government's role in education, it introduced important limitations on the functions of the local education authorities, who were forced to give greater autonomy to schools and governing bodies.
>
> (Maclure, 1988, p. ix)

Maclure singles out the national curriculum as a chief reason for an enhanced role for central government in education. The introduction of a national curriculum does indeed entail much responsibility for the secretary of state and also much work for administrators at the Department of Education and Science and for HMI. As the various working groups focusing on different aspects of the curriculum make their reports, the secretary of state has an important role in responding to their recommendations.

The Reform Act's contribution to a policy for parental choice, chiefly by promoting 'open enrolment' but in addition through the opportunity for schools to acquire grant-maintained status, also contributes to an enhanced profile for central government in education. Each school must accept pupils up to the limit of their 'standard number', the size of the school's roll in the populous days of 1979. Any school's request to deviate from that standard number is subject to a ruling by the secretary of state.[3]

There are still opportunities for individual complaints and appeals by parents seeking a place at a particular school, but here the secretary of state's intervention is less frequently called upon than in the past, since the 1980 Education Act required LEAs and the governing bodies of voluntary schools to enable parents to appeal against adverse admission decisions to specially constituted local appeal committees (Education Act, 1980, Schedule 2). To this extent, the relationship between the centre and the individual parent has become a more distanced one. But jointly, parents can, following the Reform Act, set in motion a proposal to take a school out of the local education system of which it is presently a part. Once set in train, the application for grant-maintained (as opposed to local-authority-maintained) status can only be resolved at the centre, by the secretary of state.

In the first year since the publication of the 1988 Education Reform Act, there has been a flurry of activity on the 'grant-maintained' front. Many local initiatives and counter-initiatives have been reported, only some of which have resulted in formal proposals to the secretary of state.[4] Of the proposals which have gone forward, some have been vehemently opposed by interested parties, and these objections have been considered as part of the judgement made by the Secretary of State. As noted earlier (see chapter 1, n. 32), by October 1989 27 proposals had been approved and 5 rejected, while proposals had been published for 14 more schools. Enthusiasm for the change of status may die down as time passes. Alternatively it may be heightened, either by favourable experience on the part of the new grant-maintained schools or by any adverse experience of schools remaining in LEA control where prominent local schools have withdrawn from that control. Although so far application for grant-maintained status has been piecemeal,[5] it is at least conceivable that if the new status gains widespread support as a desirable development we could eventually have a nation-wide 'system' of grant-maintained schools in which the role of the centre would be important as never before. The secretary of state, with the Department of Education and Science, would have a direct and nation-wide role in such a system.

It is also timely to reflect on the role of the centre in relation to independent schools, now that parental choice is a key element of policy. We have seen that the Assisted Places scheme, which devoted public money to the payment of school fees for children from low-income families at certain independent schools, was one of the first initiatives taken in the 1980s by a government determined to change the course of education. The scheme, introduced as part of the 1980 Education Act, has continued to expand slowly, although its impact has been overshadowed by the fundamental changes to maintained education brought about by the 1986 and 1988 Acts. To some extent the independent schools participating in the Assisted Places scheme now stand in a similar relationship to the centre as do the grant-maintained schools. There is a direct transfer of public money from the centre to those independent schools.[6]

Assisted Place schools can be seen as in some senses part of the centre's new 'empire' of schooling. If a voucher scheme were to be introduced, enabling full parental choice at public expense across the public/private sector divide, these schools would be well placed for early participation in such a scheme. At present however there are few indications that such a proposal is on the political agenda. In the whole debate preceding the passing of the Reform Act, the voucher issue was not raised. If the emphasis of government's education policy remains on diversifying maintained education and enhancing parental choice within that sector, the Assisted Place scheme is unlikely to expand further and may dwindle if the 'benefits' of private education[7] are seen by parents to be matched in the various types of maintained schools. The long-term effects of a policy of parental choice on relations between the centre and the independent schools may therefore be to ossify that relationship, if not to diminish it.

Overall, the effects of a policy favouring parental choice have been to augment the role of the centre in education, largely by making the secretary of state the key arbiter of any further proposals for change, whether these proposals emanate from parents, governing bodies or local authorities. When we turn to the effects of the policy for parental choice at the level of the LEA, we find a different outcome.

EFFECTS FOR THE LEA

As Maclure points out, the Reform Act introduced important limitations on the functions of the LEA (Maclure, 1988, p. ix). The greater autonomy which LEAs have been forced to give to schools and governing bodies cannot all be directly attributed to the policy for parental choice, but increased parental power, including the power to choose, is a corollary of that greater autonomy for schools and governors.

The requirement for local management of schools (LMS) is one aspect of the Reform Act which changes the relationship between

LEA and school. We have already seen (chapter 1) that LMS links in to parental choice, in that schools' budgets must be calculated largely on a per capita basis, providing an incentive to schools to attract pupils and keep their numbers up. Schemes for LMS are devised in negotiation between LEAs, school governing bodies and other interested parties, and subject to the final approval of the ubiquitous secretary of state.[8] They necessitate a new look at what should be treated as hard-core authority-wide responsibilities, to be retained in the authority's General Schools Budget, and what can be delegated for decision-making and handling at school level. In the early days of these negotiations about 'discretionary exceptions' to delegation, especially at the primary school level many governing bodies and headteachers were still uncertain about the extent of their new responsibilities, and their ability to cope with them. There was some tendency to acquiesce with the proposals of the LEA, and to welcome any suggestions that many aspects of the budget continue to be dealt with on an authority-wide basis. As yet it is also unclear how much autonomy schools will actually seek to exercise about staffing or admissions, which have a direct effect on their delegated budget. However it can be anticipated that as governors and teachers gain confidence they will become more adventurous in the handling of their budget, and will begin to value the financial effect of a positive school-based policy towards admissions. The LEA may come to be seen as less of a guardian and more of a rival, as it already appears to some more entrepreneurial schools.

If recourse is still had to appeal committees (as constituted by Schedule 2 of the 1980 Education Act), LEAs will need to be doubly careful that appointees match the requirements of the Act, and that the committees function as a check on the admission policies of the authorities. The work of Adler *et al.* (see chapter 3) showed that in Scotland appeals were usually decided in line with local policies, unless a further appeal was made to the sheriff. Following the Education Reform Act, appeal decisions in England[9] are likely to be keenly examined for their legality by all interested parties, since the committees will presumably be mainly asked to decide whether special circumstances justify the admission of a child or children over and above the school's standard number for admissions. Authorities can no longer have local admission policies of their own which on grounds of 'efficient use of resources' override the Reform Act's 'standard number' requirement.

Experience suggests, however, that LEAs may not all be

punctilious or speedy in implementing the requirements of the Reform Act, so far as parental choice is concerned. Research prior to the Act showed considerable resistance to parental choice, on the part of some Scottish authorities, which took the view that their role of provider of education for all was weakened by the increase of parental power (Adler *et al.*, 1987). The NFER study, discussed in chapter 3, showed that authorities in England which based their admissions on catchment area policies put forward several reasons for doing so, including the protection of unpopular schools, the promotion of community-based education, the linking of junior and secondary schools, and ease of administration (Maychell, 1986). They clearly showed the priority given to other considerations over parental choice. Even those authorities which followed an ostensibly 'open choice' policy did not always make it easy for parents to operate the choice procedure, and in some cases deliberately left the procedure vague to prevent parents 'working the system' (Maychell, 1986, p. 18). Research also showed that authorities' response to the statutory requirement of giving essential information to parents about local schools was patchy and incomplete (Maychell, 1986; Muskett, 1986). The resistant attitude of some local authorities to parental choice of school will not have been eradicated by the Reform Act, and this attitude must continue to be seen as a factor influencing the effects of the Act at the level of the LEA.

The most specific potential depletion of the authority of the LEA by the Education Reform Act lies in the opportunity for schools to transfer to grant-maintained status. While the decision of a school to opt out may or may not be seen by an LEA as a blow to its prestige, it undoubtedly means a loss of assets. If confirmed, the request for grant-maintained status means the loss of property and staff,[10] and a decrease in the funding which the LEA receives from government. Small wonder that the Reform Act devotes fifty-two sections to the subject of grant-maintained status, and that some LEAs appear to be reacting aggressively to those of their former county schools which have become grant-maintained. In August 1989 it was reported that Birmingham City Council had requested the return of 3,500 books from the school library of a grant-maintained school formerly in its control (*The Times*, 15 August 1989). This and other disputes as to what constitutes the property of a school in the terms of the Reform Act, and thus transfer to become the property of a grant-maintained school's new governing body, will be handled by the Education Assets Board, set up by

Section 197 of the 1988 Reform Act.[11] The loss of pupils is another important consideration, at a time of low numbers. In May 1989 Bedfordshire County Council appeared to be trying to divert pupils away from the grant-maintained school to which they were due to be admitted, offering them places in other county schools (*The Times*, 30 May 1989).

Some LEAs have responded amicably to schools' desire to opt out, but the future relationship between grant-maintained schools and their former LEAs will require negotiation in all cases. The break will not be a total one. Grant-maintained schools must supply necessary information and make returns to an LEA which exercises any functions in relation to the school and its registered pupils (Education Reform Act 1988, s. 103(3)), and the LEA still has the duty to provide benefits and services (such as transport and clothing) to the pupils of grant-maintained schools, and must do so 'no less favourably' than to pupils at schools maintained by the LEA (Education Reform Act 1988, s. 100).

Over and above the minor skirmishes of new relationships between the LEA and grant-maintained schools, the main effect of the extended choice to parents which these schools represent is greatly to disturb the planning function of the LEA in regard to its overall provision for the education of school-age children in the area. We saw earlier (chapter 1) that the 'planning' argument has been one of the chief objections to a policy for parental choice. During a period of falling rolls most local authorities had made plans to remove school places by closures, or to make other changes which would enable the redistribution of pupils within the authorities' schools.[12] Several of the first wave of applications for grant-maintained status were from schools liable to closure by the LEA. Any such application 'freezes' any proposals which the LEA may have in hand to close or make significant changes in the character or premises of the school, and the LEA may not formulate any such proposals (under s. 12(1)(c) or (d) of the 1980 Act) without now notifying the governing body of 'any school which is eligible for grant-maintained status' (Education Reform Act 1988, s. 73(1)). In other words, most schools faced with closure or (as they perceive it), undesirable change, can put on the discussion table the possibility of a request to opt out from the control of the LEA making the proposal. Not only county schools but also voluntary aided schools have found this a useful move, as will be discussed below.

EFFECTS FOR THE DIOCESE

Reference in this section is to the body or bodies which give administrative backing and in some cases policy guidance to the voluntary aided school. 'The diocese' is a convenient umbrella term to denote these bodies, but it is not a strictly accurate one in all cases. Jewish voluntary aided schools have no 'diocesan' network behind them, only the foundation or trust which established them. Nevertheless they stand apart from county schools in that they are affiliated to some kind of group or body separate from the LEA. Church of England and Roman Catholic voluntary aided schools are affiliated to much more conspicuous sub-systems, the Anglican and Catholic churches. Duncan (1989) points out that both the Church of England and the Roman Catholic Church are episcopal churches with a diocesan network. He claims that, although the Church of England is the established church of the land, both it and the Roman Catholic Church can be seen as 'national churches in the sense that their schools could be, indeed should be, perceived as agents or representatives of the wider Church at both the national and diocesan level, as well as being very much part of the local scene' (Duncan, 1989). Indeed one could go further and bring in the international dimension, in that, as we saw in chapter 2, Roman Catholic schools are part of a world-wide church and receive guidance from the Vatican, via the Catholic Truth society.

For this discussion it is sufficient to recognize a possible separation between the interests of the voluntary aided school as an institution, and the interests of some wider entity such as the diocese. A policy for parental choice – and in particular the opportunity to opt for grant-maintained status – has the potential to emphasize that separation and to reveal the tensions which exist between the two sets of interests. The case of the Cardinal Vaughan School is illustrative.

In 1987 the Catholic diocese of Westminster, headed by Cardinal Hume, Archbishop of Westminster and the Trustee of the Cardinal Vaughan School, a voluntary aided secondary school for boys, put forward a plan to reorganize Catholic education in the diocese. The plan made the not unusual proposal to separate off 16 plus education from the secondary schools, setting up a sixth form college. Trustee (or 'foundation') governors who had sons at the Cardinal Vaughan School opposed the diocesan plan. They were dismissed by the Archbishop. Many parents of boys at Cardinal Vaughan School did not want the school to lose its sixth form. Early in 1989 an official ballot of all parents voted strongly to seek grant-maintained status, which would take them beyond the scope of the diocesan plan.[13]

These parents were not the first to see grant-maintained status as a way of serving the interests of the school as an institution, in opposition to the expressed wishes of the diocese. One of the first schools to receive grant-maintained status was a Church of England aided secondary school in a diocese which was one of the few to have an explicit Diocesan Education Committee policy against opting out (Duncan, 1989). However Cardinal Vaughan parents, in using the 'opting out' tactic, were temporarily out-manoeuvred by the Archbishop. The governing body of a school must prepare and submit detailed proposals for becoming a grant-maintained school before the secretary of state can legally consider them. Archbishop Hume held up consideration of the application for grant-maintained status by refusing to appoint the foundation governors needed to make up the governing body.

Eventually an appeal court decided that the trustee could not dismiss governors he had appointed. In August 1989 the Archbishop agreed to 'use his best endeavours' to find suitable people to serve on the governing body as foundation governors, and by October 1989 proposals for the acquisition of grant-maintained status had been published. The diocese has shown itself unable to act positively to impede the wishes of parents in seeking grant-maintained status, although it is still of course possible that the secretary of state will reject the proposals, taking account of the objection of the Trustee or others (Education Reform Act 1988, s. 62(10)).

Controversies such as this, assiduously reported in the press, show that a policy for parental choice can test the limits of diocesan power. The Church of England has for some years had in hand a draft measure emphasizing the valid interests of a diocese in issues wider than those which are local to particular schools. The measure, which has been adopted by the General Synod[14] but still requires approval by Parliament, would not enable the diocese to block a move for a school to become grant-maintained, but it would require the school to seek the advice of the diocese on the matter and 'have regard' to its advice. The local versus diocesan tension is being heightened by the Education Reform Act and its policies for parental choice.

Apart from the possible divergence between the organizational plans of the diocese for all its voluntary aided schools, and the interests of a particular school, there is another aspect of grant-maintained status which could threaten the interests of the diocese, as it does for the LEA in the case of county schools. This is the question of the transfer of assets which grant-maintained status entails.

If a voluntary aided school is closed for any reason, the proceeds from the sale of the property (which was provided in the first instance and externally maintained by the Trust) can, in the case of Church of England or Roman Catholic schools, be recycled throughout the diocese to benefit other aided schools. Duncan (1989) points out that the locality may oppose the diocese in this, but such conflicts are not part of our consideration here of the effects of policies for parental choice. However, if a voluntary aided school achieves grant-maintained status, as an asset it passes out of the hands of the diocese. The requirement for the governors to meet fifteen per cent of certain maintenance costs no longer applies. The Reform Act devotes several sections to the elucidation of what happens if a grant-maintained school subsequently closes or is closed by the secretary of state (Reform Act 1988, ss 94–101). So far as the disposal of assets is concerned, much appears to depend on what subsequent use is to be made of the premises. No experience of actual cases is likely to be available for some years. For our purposes the point is that it is no longer in the remit of the diocese to close such a school as part of a diocesan plan, and use the proceeds to benefit other aided schools.

Closures of grant-maintained schools are, it can be assumed, a distant eventuality. Of more immediate interest is the relationship which becomes established between the diocesan or equivalent body and the formerly voluntary aided school which becomes grant-maintained. Maclure (1988, p. 76) suggests that if grant-maintained schools enjoy high prestige, the Churches will be forced to come to terms with the fact that they will be popular with their lay people, and are likely to drop their oppositional attitude to such schools.

Choice and the schools

When we look at the effect of a policy for parental choice on schools it is, as with the effect on sub-systems of education, difficult to separate one effect of the Reform Act from another. The introduction of local management of finance immediately causes schools to look at one another in a different way, to see which schools 'gain' and which 'lose' by the formula employed. Initial gains and losses were related to the difference between average staff costs used in the formula and the actual cost of paying existing teachers who have reached particular points in the incremental scale. Once these adjustments have been worked through (usually with a phasing-in of the formula over several years) schools may begin to compare themselves with other schools on matters more related to parental choice. For example, differences may be perceived in the opportunities which some schools appear to have to enrol pupils of a calibre which gives the school a good reputation, and attracts additional families to the school by a 'multiplier' effect. It will become important for other schools to analyse how those opportunities come about. Are they created by some deliberate strategy on the part of the 'fortunate' school? Can they be competed with?

All this is surmise for the future. But if we look again at some of the findings from Whitty, Fitz and Edwards' Assisted Place study (Edwards *et al.*, 1989), we can see examples of how maintained and independent schools related to one another in a competitive situation, examples which are pointers to the effects on the interrelationships of maintained schools now that parental choice is becoming the key to survival and, perhaps, prosperity in the sense of an enlarged school budget.

From the outset, the Assisted Place study showed the strength of feeling with which some headteachers and staff opposed the very notion of competition between schools. These were schools which, on principle, refused all access to the research team (see chapter 4). This 'abhorrence' of competition in education, as one maintained-school head expressed it to the Assisted Place research team, is likely to be a continuing attitude of some providers of maintained education, and may make it difficult for them to cooperate with a policy of parental choice which looks to a market ideology. Equality of opportunity for all pupils, as we saw in chapter 1, has long been an important value in education. For some, equality of opportunity and a market orientation in education seem incompatible. A distaste for competition is a real feature of some teachers' attitude to their professional life, which cannot be ignored when considering the effects of a policy for parental choice. In schools where it is felt to be unacceptable to assess the strengths of other schools and vie with them for pupils in a competitive way, an alternative may be to attempt to foster loyalty among families with children already on roll, and perhaps to stress the place of the school in the life of the locality. The notion of the 'community' school is already established in some areas, but some tension between the ethos of a community school and a policy for free parental choice has been perceived (Bastiani, 1988). Community schools look to a 'neighbourhood' of participating families, an idea which fitted with a catchment area system for the allocation of pupils. Now, a policy of more open enrolment might mean that parents would make use of a community school for their own leisure and study needs, but send their children elsewhere. Engendering loyalty and a sense of membership may become the overriding goal for a community school.

Another factor affecting the way schools conduct themselves in an atmosphere of competition is the past history of educational provision in the area. There is no *tabula rasa* for the introduction of a policy of parental choice. Schools in some localities, as the Assisted Place research team found, may have long perceived themselves as having a particular place in a hierarchy of schools, and will not readily re-define the situation as one in which families will be influenced in their choice solely by the present-day amenities and achievements of each school (nor indeed will the parents – a point we shall return to later).

One effect of the pressures of parental choice may be on inter-professional relations between teachers in a locality. Whitty and Edwards found that some secondary schools would have no dealings with independent schools offering Assisted Places, and if grant-maintained schools are seen as similarly unwelcome competitors for local children, there may be some estrangement between teachers at LEA and grant-maintained schools. The Assisted Place research also found some antagonism between primary and secondary headteachers in the maintained sector, in cases where primary heads were giving advice to parents about particular secondary schools, whether maintained or independent. The influence of primary heads on parental decisions about secondary schooling may become increasingly resented by secondary headteachers, in an atmosphere of competition to enrol pupils.

In Scotland, Adler *et al.* concluded that in certain areas parental choice was leading to a polarization of popular and unpopular schools. If the Reform Act's provisions increase this polarization tendency, some schools may find they can no longer rely on retaining the 'critical mass' of able pupils which, in the Assisted Places study, were defined as crucial in keeping a school buoyant. Although this research team found that the competition provided by Assisted Place schools was not stimulating high grade comprehensive schools to any further efforts to better themselves, the wider competition entailed by increased parental choice within the maintained sector may have the effect of stimulating even well-established schools into greater efforts to enhance their local reputation. It may be that all schools will seek to stress their capacity to educate children of overall high ability. Alternatively, and perhaps especially if LEAs encourage the notion of variety rather than uniformity of provision within their area, individual schools may try to become 'magnets' for pupils with particular talents or particular needs. Independent schools, through their public relations arm ISIS, have tried to temper the abrasive image of direct competition by stressing that they aim to complement, rather than supplant, the schools of the maintained sector. This notion of complementarity within the maintained sector itself, with each school providing something slightly different from the others, might enable maintained schools to continue to live together in relative harmony, in the new era of parental choice.

Choice and the parents

All the researchers whose work was discussed in chapters 3 and 4 devoted some resources to examining how and why parents attempt to choose schools for their children, but it cannot be claimed that the processes of parental choice are now fully understood. Certain issues have emerged, however, which can be the basis for conjecture on how the new emphasis on parental choice of school will work through into consumer behaviour.

PARENTAL EXPECTATIONS ABOUT CHOICE

Over the last twenty-five years there has been a gradual increase in parents' perceptions that they have the right to choose their child's school, and their efforts to exercise that right. While at the time of the Plowden enquiry (Central Advisory Council for Education, England, 1967) over fifty per cent of parents thought they could have made a choice but only six per cent actually tried to do so, the

Edinburgh study in the 1980s found the great majority of parents knew that recent Scottish legislation entitled them to make a placing request, and an average of eleven per cent had done so in the areas studied. Wide local variations were found in the incidence of placing requests, and in some areas this opportunity for choice was taken by more families at the primary than at the secondary stage (see chapter 3).

Stillman and Maychell (1986) (the NFER study) found that in England too parents' sense of being able to make a choice varied in different areas. Certainly the motivation to make a choice or to pursue a choice by appeal appears to be linked to local educational circumstances, but research has not clearly established what features create a sense of choice. In some areas it was the presence of voluntary schools alongside local authority schools, but in other cases parents felt they had a real choice between apparently similar schools provided both were within reasonable travelling distance.

Whatever it is that creates a sense of choice for parents (and local authority attitudes in setting out the options, discussed earlier in this chapter, must surely be a contributory feature), there seems no doubt that if parents feel they have a genuine choice they will put time and effort into making that choice. If choice is rejected and an appeal becomes necessary, this can be a formidable barrier for parents, who may have no previous experience of dealings with the LEA (Johnson and Ransom, 1983) and may moreover find it hard to distinguish between appeal committee members and LEA officers (Tweedie *et al.*, 1986). However, if choice is successful, several researchers including myself have found that family commitment to the school of choice seems high (Stillman and Maychell, 1986; Johnson, 1987).

Research before the Reform Act therefore suggests that parental expectations about being able to make a choice will have been further increased by the new legislation and attendant publicity, but that the actual exercise of choice, although proportionately increased, will still be influenced by local educational circumstances and the attitude taken by the LEA.

CRITERIA FOR CHOICE

We saw in chapters 3 and 4 that there are problems in establishing, through research with parents, what criteria they apply in the choice of school for their child. If researchers ask open-ended questions, leaving it to parents to say in their own words how they choose schools, the result may be a wide range of highly individual accounts, which are hard to classify. If on the other hand parents are asked to choose from, or place in ranked order, a list of criteria put forward by the researcher, there is a distinct possibility that an important criterion is missing from the list, or that parents will tailor their replies to fit the alternatives available. The research discussed earlier supplied examples of both approaches. Despite the drawbacks of both methods, these studies do, between them, provide a reasonably coherent account of the range of considerations on which parental choice of school is based.

It is clear that choice is a complex process, and that families have more than one reason for favouring a particular school. Research such as Stillman and Maychell's (1986) that shows the combination of reasons mentioned gives a better picture of family decision-making than enquiries which simply collate the number of mentions of a given criterion by all the parents interviewed (University of Glasgow, 1986). Elliott's (1981a) idea of separating product and process criteria was an interesting form of analysis, but most families seem to set store by both the outcomes *and* the day-to-day experience of schooling for their children. The elusive quality of 'happiness' at school is highly valued, and this is surely a 'process' criterion. But being 'happy' at school may include 'doing well academically' (as Petch (1986) surmised), an experience which whilst satisfying in itself may also have 'product' type outcomes, in the form of examination success leading to rewarding employment. Several researchers have found that parents value 'discipline' at the school of their choice, and this is usually defined as a process criterion related to the experience of being at the particular school. But Fox (1985) elicited from the parents of public schoolboys that a well-disciplined school life was valued for them as a way of 'learning to live in world that has rules'. Once again outcome and process seem inseparable. We can only conclude, without surprise, that parents choosing schools for their children will have in mind both what it will be like for them to spend several years in daily contact with the school as an institution, and also what long-term effects their schooling will have on their later life. Which aspect is given most emphasis will depend on many other factors, among them the age and temperament of the child and his or her inclinations, as demonstrated in leisure activities or family relations.[15]

Influential factors are not all exclusively child-centred, however. Family circumstances, family convenience, and how comfortable parents feel about the school their child will attend have been found to be prominent in families' assessment of a suitable school. The many families who send their child to a school they themselves, or a near relative, attended, even though the organization of the school may have changed considerably in the intervening years, demonstrate that some degree of familiarity lessens the constraint which many adults still feel when required to have dealings with the professional world of school. Recent research by Limerick (1989) has shown that fringe members of Australian society, such as the unemployed, and poorly educated women, find considerable satisfaction in voluntary helping-out at the local school (Johnson, 1990). The extent to which involvement with a school will prove therapeutic or enjoyable for the parents cannot necessarily be known or influential at the time of choosing a school for a child, but how the parents feel about the school as a place they have to have some dealings with is important. It is the other side of the relationship from the headmaster who did not want the child if he did not like the parents he would have to work with (see chapter 4). In studying the take-up of the Assisted Places scheme, the research team were at first surprised and faintly disapproving that the scheme has attracted one-parent families made 'artificially' poor by divorce, bereavement or unemployment. However, they came to feel sympathy with the pride of parents in difficult circumstances that their child was attending an elite school (Edwards *et al.*, 1989, p. 157). It is not hard to envisage the satisfaction which association with a prestigious school might afford to a family deprived by unanticipated loss of various kinds, or the feeling which a parent might have that the 'extra' input from society which an Assisted Place represents could compensate a child for the loss of certain other benefits in life. Psychological considerations of this kind can scarcely be taken on board by policy-makers, but they are an element in the consumer behaviour which makes use of policy.

The location of schools (labelled 'geography' in the NFER study) is an important aspect of family convenience and its influence on choice. Some choices are ruled out because the desired type of school does not exist in the locality.[16] Several research studies (Johnson and Ransom, 1983; Petch, 1986; University of Glasgow, 1986) showed that parents were unwilling for their children to undertake complicated journeys to school, journeys which might be costly, tiring or dangerous. Nevertheless, Whitty and Edwards (Edwards *et al.*, 1989) found that the existence of competition between schools prompted a re-definition of 'the locality'. Both independent and maintained schools were marketing, and drawing their pupils from, a wider area than hitherto. Families too may enlarge their horizons if they become newly aware of attractive schools which, although further away, are still within a feasible distance for daily travel. The 'nearness to home' criterion for choice may prove negotiable.

Some families seem to make only one set of choice decisions, for their first child, and thereafter subsequent children follow the same educational paths. Parents' choice of a school for their first child may be based on a number of reasons concerning either the child or the school. Later in family life convenience becomes a more central criterion, and it proves easiest for brothers and sisters to join the same school. Home–school relations are confined to a single institution, and travelling to and fro on a daily basis is simplified if all the children have the same destination. LEAs have always recognized this 'family convenience' factor, and almost all admission policies preceding the Reform Act gave high priority to families with a child already on the roll of the school. It is of course also possible that several children from a family joining the same school demonstrate the satisfaction of parents with their first child's experience at the school, but occasionally family convenience may override even adverse experience (Johnson and Ransom, 1983). Weariness with the need to exercise choice may also become a factor. Most children attend at least three schools, and if choice is consciously exercised on each occasion, the prospect of similar decision-making on behalf of several more children could seem irksome. My research with families who used both private schools and state schools (Johnson, 1987) showed that some parents remain zestful decision-makers about schooling right through to the end of a large family, but this enthusiasm may not be widespread. One of the great unknowns of the effects of a policy emphasizing parental choice is the extent to which parents will want to exercise that choice, both for their first and subsequent children.

Choices made for a first child can also be influential in the lives of younger brothers and sisters for reasons of 'fairness', a very important feature of family decision-making. My research showed that when one child is moved from the public to the private sector of education, often for very specific child-centred reasons, there was a domino effect in the family, with subsequent children following the same route. Parents who had paid fees for one child seemed to feel they should do the same for other children, even in the face of financial hardship (Johnson, 1987). Even where fees are not involved, it may be that families who spend money on enabling one child to travel to a school outside their immediate locality – perhaps a grant-maintained school – will feel constrained to draw on the family budget similarly for other children.

None of the criteria for choice so far referred to seem likely to be specially affected by a heightened policy for parental choice. However, we saw earlier that local educational circumstances influence the ways in which schools respond to an emphasis on choice. Similarly for parents, local educational circumstances have an effect on how choice is exercised, and the Reform Act is likely to bring about change in those circumstances in a number of ways.

Parents' own education was affected by educational policies prevailing in the past, and the local circumstances which these produced. We saw in chapter 4 that some parents were influenced to seek private education for their children by memories of free places in direct grant and other grammar schools, a type of education which was now only available to them locally by the payment of fees. Some parents encountered in the same study (Johnson, 1987) also bemoaned the ending of secondary technical schools, from which they themselves had benefited. City technology colleges may be perceived by some parents as an updated revival of this kind of technical education, and grant-maintained schools may well seem to be the successors of the former direct grant schools. These new creations of the Education Reform Act may have a powerful attraction for some parents not solely on the basis of their present-day qualities, but because of their apparent similarity to valued schools of the past. However some families may feel that the advent of these forms of education narrows rather than widens their choice between local schools. The debate which preceded the Reform Act showed that some LEAs feared that opting out by certain popular schools would reduce the range of educational choices they could offer to local families (Haviland, 1988). If parents see grant-maintained status as making schools so 'special' that they are outside the orbit of ordinary families (as some perceived the direct grant schools to be, in the past), then their sense of choice will be diminished rather than enlarged by the effects of the Reform Act. Equally, for some families in the past, secondary technical schools were always perceived as the 'poor relation' of grammar schools, and city technology colleges may seem unattractive because of that historical residue. However, given the public and private resources on which the colleges are able to draw, this seems unlikely.[17]

Even in areas where no opting out occurs, and no city technology colleges are established, local education circumstances are likely to be changed by the Reform Act, and parents' criteria for choice may be affected. The more positive marketing of schools which 'open' enrolment and LMS seem to encourage may make schools appear much more varied than the previous low-key 'information' about local schools from the LEA had given parents reason to believe. Some parents in the 1980s wanted to send their children to a school with a clear *raison d'etre* (Johnson, 1987). Suddenly it may seem that *all* schools demonstrate this clarity of purpose, and the differences between them may be evident. Edwards *et al.* (1989) found that where variety is available, not only is parents' sense of choice generally increased, but they also begin to set more store by particular criteria such as high quality academic teaching. Parents' expectations about education and what it can achieve may well be raised, and they may expect much more from schools on a number of different fronts, if local educational circumstances are transformed by competitive marketing.

Some politicians have long had the impression that parents choose, or would like to choose, secondary schools on the basis of their examination results, and should have full access to information about these. Whether or not these measures of academic success have in the past been important influences on parental choice of school (Gray, 1981; Gray, McPherson and Raffe, 1983; Ranson *et al.*, 1986), a heightened atmosphere of choice may lead parents to evaluate schools on this basis in the future, along with many of the other criteria already discussed which will continue to be influential on families' choice of school following the Reform Act, as they were in earlier years.

One further criterion of school choice remains to be discussed: the preference of the child concerned. How is this likely to be affected by a policy for parental choice? Although we have seen in chapter 1 that some writers consider parental choice devalues children and makes them the pawns of adult decision-making (David, 1978; Baron *et al.*, 1981), there is little evidence that parents choosing schools disregard the wishes of their child. Coons and Sugarman (1978) preferred to speak of 'family' choice, and although this is not the phrase used in the United Kingdom legislation, most of the available research suggests that choice of school is usually a family affair. However, no research has focused specifically on the criteria which potential pupils bring to bear, when expressing a preference for a particular school. It is generally assumed that the experience of older brothers or sisters, or the intentions of existing school friends, are what influence children to want to go to certain local schools. In my earlier research with working-class families (Johnson and Ransom, 1983) I came across one or two examples of young people who had masterminded their own educational careers without any reference to family experience or local custom, and persuaded their parents to back their choice, but these were rare cases. Most children seemed content to follow the crowd, or to go to the school chosen for the eldest child in the family, whether or not that child was particularly happy at the school.

The question of schoolchildren's influence on choice is naturally most relevant at the time of transfer from primary to secondary school, when they already have some experience of being a school pupil. In 'open choice' areas, where primary schools commonly dispersed their pupils to a number of different secondary schools, and especially when some pupils habitually transferred to the private sector, my research in the 1980s which mapped the school careers of the seventy-two children of twenty-five families (Johnson, 1987), suggested that children's readiness to participate in choice, like their parents', was strengthened by awareness of a wide range of schools, and the expectation that a positive choice must be made, rather than awaiting an LEA allocation decision. Some examples were even found of children who had been the first instigators of a move to the private sector, although in all such cases children had of course needed to enlist the support of their potentially fee-paying parents.

It is of interest that the one piece of research that attempts to evaluate the influence of 'children's friends' on school choice (Edwards *et al.*, 1989) found that this factor was rather less important in family choices leading to Assisted Places than it was for families choosing other forms of education. This is probably because of the essentially individualized nature of the procedures entailed in application for, and award of, an Assisted Place. It could be that a voucher system, extending across public and private education, would lead to similarly individualized decision-making, taking little account of the proposed school destinations of children's friends. However, there seems no reason to suppose that the more modest provisions of the Reform Act for enhanced parental choice will lead either to the increase or the decrease of participation in family decision-making about choice of school by the child concerned.

Conclusion

The effects of a policy for parental choice cannot be entirely separated from the effects of other policies also introduced by the wide-ranging Education Reform Act of 1988. It is evident, however, that the introduction of new forms of education about which choice can be expressed – grant-maintained schools and city colleges of various kinds – shakes up existing relationships between centre and sub-systems, and between sub-systems and their component institutions. Local education authorities in particular are entering a new era, and only time will tell whether the requirement to enable local management of schools, or a combination of the parental choice possibilities popularly referred to as 'opting out and open enrolment', will present LEAs with the greater challenge.

For schools of all kinds, the main imperative arising from parental choice is to establish a viable attitude to competition. County, voluntary and independent schools have always been in competition for the same school-age group of young people, but in some areas market shares have been tacitly divided between them by local custom and administrative arrangements. County schools in particular, sheltered by the allocative arrangements of the LEA, have often been able to ignore the existence of competitors. Now the emphasis on parental choice means that the issue must be faced. For those professionals who believe overt competition and sound education to be incompatible, competitive activities must be somehow sublimated into ideas of service to the local community, or other acceptable aims. In other cases, a more openly entrepreneurial attitude to competition will prove viable, and may indeed mean only a sharpening of attitudes which already exist. But in all cases, schools now have to recognize what some of them have always known, that the supply of pupils to schools is not a predetermined 'ration' of a scarce or plentiful resource, but the result of many individual acts of family choice.

The effects of choice for parents cannot readily be summarized. The many criteria for choice to which families refer show that in their own minds at least parents and children have always identified preferences for particular schools or types of schooling. Some families have been able to make these preferences prevail, either because they were in line with local custom and allocative practice, or because the families had the financial or social resources to make their views count. Now, all parents of school-age children have an enhanced opportunity to make effective choices in education. For individual families this may be a welcome change. Whether new pressures of parental demand may also bring about change in the forms of supply of schooling is discussed in the next chapter.

Chapter 6

Choice as a factor in educational change

Earlier discussion of the scope of choice showed that there are many different kinds of schooling (see chapter 2). But are parents more likely to seek out any of these options – for residential rather than day schools, single-sex rather than coeducational schools, selective rather than non-selective schools and so on – as a result of the Education Reform Act and its emphasis on choice? Research into choice has not tended to focus on these particular alternatives, but does give some pointers to ways in which some of these options may seem more attractive to parents in an atmosphere of choice. Discussion here will consider the position of voluntary schools, girls' schools, and academically selective schools, in an era of parental choice.

Voluntary schools

Voluntary schools are an option which has been demonstrably attractive to parents in the past, but an emphasis on choice seems to throw up different reasons for these schools' popularity, some of which may be interactive with choice, so that the schools become subtly different institutions.

As we saw in chapter 2, voluntary schools were incorporated into the maintained sector of education to satisfy the wishes of their founders, and the perceived wishes of families of various religious persuasions, for public education to include schools which provided opportunities for particular forms of worship and religious teaching. In the 1980s, the most important providers of voluntary schools were the Roman Catholic and Anglican churches.[1]

Catholic schools, as we have seen, were established to provide a nation-wide opportunity for specifically Catholic education, and Cardinal Hume has affirmed that the provision of a national network of schools is still a basic part of the Catholic Church's strategy (*The Times*, 6 September 1989. Report by Clifford Longley). Although the schools work in relative harmony with local education authorities, they have not tended to keep pace with organizational changes occurring in local county schools. Accordingly some Catholic secondary schools have been seen (and valued) by parents as survivals from an earlier era, when single-sex, academically oriented, secondary education was more prevalent. In choosing a Catholic secondary school for their children, practising Catholic parents have not had to clarify, either to themselves or to others, whether the school's religious orientation was what they most valued about it, or whether its form of organization, curriculum and disciplinary ethos were equally or more important. Now, the opportunity to 'opt out', and the particular case of the Cardinal Vaughan school, has shown that some parents find it more important to preserve the character of the individual school, than to acquiesce in wider plans to meet what the diocese sees as the needs and requirements of the local Catholic community as a whole.

This episode, and other 'systematic attempts inside the Catholic church in Britain to encourage opting out . . . as a way of escaping the consequence of diocesan schemes'[2] appear to confirm what some observers have long claimed (Socialist Educational Association, 1981), that part of the appeal of voluntary schools for parents is their tendency to differ from the normal run of maintained schools, in aspects *other* than the religious. My own research (Johnson, 1987) found examples of practising Church of England families who were interested in sending their children to voluntary-aided schools *not* because of any religious teaching (which they thought was better imparted by home and church) but because of the fairly formal disciplinary style of a voluntary-aided primary school, or the academic tradition of a voluntary-aided secondary school. Much more research will be needed fully to uncover the significance of voluntary schools for those who choose them, but enough is known to appreciate why in some of the localities examined by Edwards *et al.* (1989) the presence of voluntary schools increased parents' sense of choice. Voluntary schools *do* seem different, in ways other than the purely religious.

However, in the choice-affirming atmosphere of re-formed

education, there is also renewed emphasis on the potential for voluntary schools to impart religious teaching. Some Muslim parents prefer a voluntary aided to a county school because of its anticipated religious ethos, even if the religious teaching is not that of Islam. Some Church of England voluntary school headteachers have such a high proportion of Muslims on roll that they feel it inappropriate to stress Christian affiliations and find that even a multicultural approach seems unsuited to an almost exclusively Muslim pupil population. This situation is another example of choice being interactive with the characteristics of a school, making it a rather different institution. In the case of Headfield (voluntary controlled) middle school in Dewsbury, the school became unpopular with non-Muslim parents because it was no longer perceived as a Christian school (and no doubt for other reasons).[3]

There are, it is clear, simultaneous pressures on voluntary schools to be both more and less religious, and these pressures are rendered more noticeable by an atmosphere of choice. There is also pressure group activity campaigning for an entirely new category of voluntary aided school, for Muslims (see chapter 2 for an earlier brief discussion of this development). British Islam, unlike British Jewry, does tend to encourage converts, and there are a growing number of English Muslims. However, the great majority of Muslims living in Britain are of Asian origin, and Islamic voluntary aided schools have so far chiefly been refused on the grounds that they would encourage racial separation in education.[4] There is also some apprehension that for religious and cultural reasons Islamic girls could not receive the same educational opportunities in an Islamic voluntary aided school as they would in a county school or a Christian or Jewish voluntary aided school.

It is not yet clear whether pressure in favour of Muslim voluntary schools comes primarily from Muslim parents or from religious leaders. However research into 'Muslim pupils in British schools' currently taking place in Birmingham, includes interviews with parents, to be conducted by Gujerati- and Hindi-speaking interviewers. It is hoped that these interviews will throw some light on the school choices that Muslim parents themselves would prefer to make.[5]

Overall, it seems that the choice of a voluntary school is one kind of choice which parents will continue to try to exercise in the post-Reform-Act era, but this choice will be made for a number of different reasons, some of which may nudge individual schools in diverging directions.

Schools for girls

Another option to which some of the research discussed made fleeting reference was that of single-sex schooling. Whitty and Edwards (Edwards *et al.*, 1989) told of a school which seemed to be valued primarily for its 'girls' only' intake. My own research (Johnson, 1987) showed that for some parents the gender-related admission policy of a girls' school seemed to be the main foundation for its popularity. That both these single-sex schools were for girls, not boys, is perhaps no coincidence. Boys' schools which admit a few girls do not seem to be changed by this experience, and indeed one boys' independent school (Belmont Abbey School, Hereford) which admitted girls to the sixth form for a few years has decided to phase out this experiment, since it was concluded that the girls were disadvantaged in what remained an indubitably male environment.[6] Coeducation might be expected to (and some would claim, does) provide a balanced educational environment in which both boys and girls have an equal opportunity to feel at ease, but some research (Shaw, 1980, 1984; Deem, 1984) has fuelled a dispute that in coeducational schools boys dominate classroom discussion and monopolize equipment, to the detriment of girls' academic progress. Girls' schools in the 1980s have ruled out the admission of even a small number of boys. The schools stress the opportunity they provide for girls to establish their priorities and develop their abilities in a separate all-girl environment.

The trend in schooling has nevertheless been away from single-sex institutions and towards coeducation. Equal Opportunities legislation has had the unanticipated effect of reinforcing this trend. LEAs which have more single-sex school places for boys than girls are in breach of the legislation, and some have sought to solve their problem by proposing the amalgamation of boys' and girls' schools. It seems unlikely that arguments about the educational advantages of separate schools would suffice to maintain girls' schools as a viable choice for many families, were it not for other arguments in their favour. Many families, including, again, Muslim families, for religious and cultural reasons prefer their adolescent girls to grow up in a mainly female setting. For fundamentalist Muslim families this is, indeed, an absolute requirement, and we saw earlier (chapter 1, n. 3), that families boycotted the coeducational school to which their daughters were allocated, to show their unyielding opposition to mixed-sex secondary education.

Undoubtedly single-sex schools for girls are one kind of choice which some families will expect to be able to make, in the post-Reform-Act era. It will be interesting to see whether pressure is sufficient to persuade some schools and LEAs to change their mixed-sex intake policies, in response to parental choice.

Academically selective schools

A third option which parents, given an increased opportunity to make their preferences count, may wish to see more readily available in the maintained sector, is the choice of academically selective schooling. This is an extremely sensitive issue. The possibility of a widespread return to schooling in ability-segregated groups is so out of phase with post-1944 educational developments as to be almost a proscribed subject for academic (as opposed to political) discussion. However, it will be tackled here. We will consider first the possibility that parents may be looking for something more differentiated than comprehensive schooling at the secondary stage, before turning to the even more controversial topic of streaming by ability in primary schools.

From the outset it must be said that there is no unequivocal evidence that the majority of parents do not want comprehensive secondary education for their children. However, there is no strong contrary evidence that they do want such schools. The long debate, and the many political and administrative battles which have accompanied the process of comprehensivization in secondary schools over the past thirty years, have chiefly been waged by politicians, both locally and nationally, as well as by educationalists and academics. The voice of parents has certainly not been silent, but most organized parental lobbying on both sides of the argument has been by politically affiliated parents, or 'parent' pressure groups which are so closely in harmony with teachers that an exclusively parental viewpoint is hard to identify, if indeed it exists. Many teachers are, after all, parents, and vice versa. Why does it nevertheless seem a possibility that increased opportunities for parental choice, following the Education Reform Act, may reveal a widespread preference for ability-segregated secondary schooling?

First, there is the fact that academically selective secondary schooling has never entirely disappeared from the maintained sector. Some LEAs have retained grammar schools and not been deterred from doing so by the minority in which they find themselves. Local opinion, with few exceptions, has tended to value the presence of these schools and there has been no continued concerted outcry against the procedures which decide the allocation of children to these and other maintained schools. The remaining grammar schools are the closest competitors of the independent schools, but for the most part it is the independent sector which makes a feature of academic selection, in its most prestigious schools. Rae (1981) contends that independent schools have become much less 'comprehensive', and more fiercely academically oriented, since the maintained sector offered them this market opportunity by turning to all-ability schools.

Comprehensive schools have their critics. The main unease expressed has been fear of a lowering of standards, though this has not been unequivocally supported by research. Whitty, Fitz and Edwards have focused their whole Assisted Place study around arguments about 'the academic costs associated with comprehensive education, and the social costs associated with academic selection' (Whitty *et al.*, 1989). This debate cannot be entered into here. Our question is whether parental choice will be seen by parents as an opportunity to show support for, and demand the extension of, an educational feature which is presently out of fashion, the separation of children into academically differentiated schools, a system which characterized public secondary education for some sixty years.[7]

The fact that existing academically-selective schools, whether in the maintained or independent sectors, are almost always oversubscribed, does not necessarily mean that families who choose these schools are opposed to comprehensive education. This issue was the motive for Fox's study of families using boys' public schools, but she did not uncover a particular antipathy to all-ability schooling. Rather, these families seemed to have abandoned the maintained sector, as an area of schooling for which they had no concern (Fox, 1984, 1985). Some of the families I interviewed (Johnson, 1987) certainly chose independent education because there were no longer any maintained grammar schools in their area, but many other reasons for moving between state and private education were revealed by the research, as we saw in chapter 4.

It is impossible to say whether the many families who apply for Assisted Places, or present their children for competitive entry to independent schools, have primarily in mind the academic selectivity of these schools or other attributes which they perceive in them. What is more certain is that primary school headteachers do advise some parents to send their children to academically selective secondary schools in the area, where they exist, and that parents find this advice persuasive (Edwards *et al.*, 1989). Whitty and Edwards also found that where a sense of choice is experienced, interest in academic standards is one of the ideas aroused. Competitive academic entry procedures are one of the most visible ways in which a school can demonstrate its interest in such standards.[8] However, schools of the academically-selective type do *not* exist in all areas, and there may well be an unsatisfied demand for places at such schools which the encouragement of parental choice will bring to the surface.

Whether parents might also like to choose primary schools where children are not taught in mixed-ability groups is an even more speculative question. The issue of parental choice of primary education has been largely neglected in the research literature, and primary schools have not so far been prominent in reported cases of educational upheaval in the post-Reform-Act era of parental choice. Primary schools of 300 pupils or more are eligible for grant-maintained status, but, to date, none has applied for it.[9] Nevertheless, primary education in the maintained sector has not been entirely free from controversy during the 1970s and 1980s. Debate has focused mainly on progressive versus traditional forms of teaching (Bennett, 1976). Reliance on the perceived 'readiness' of children to tackle new problems has been queried by writers from different viewpoints who consider that child-centred teaching either does not extend children or does not focus equally on all children (Bantock, 1969; Sharp and Green, 1975). The child-centred, progressive approach was part of the argument for the abolition of ability streaming in primary schools in the 1960s (Jackson, 1964; Chanan, 1970; Lunn, 1970). One of the most uncomfortable findings of my own research into families' intermittent use of private education (Johnson, 1987) was the considerable disenchantment of some families with the maintained primary schools that their children had formerly attended. Mixed-ability teaching did not appear to be working well in these schools, and able children were being held back until the least able in the group were 'ready' for the next reading book or the next project.

These pointers may say more about the difficulties which some teachers experience in handling mixed-ability groups in the primary classroom than they do about a positive parental wish for a return to ability streaming at the primary stage. But if there is any groundswell of preference for this old-style practice, it could increase in the new climate of parental choice, as parents begin to realize that schools are in competition for their children, and may be ready to consider whether parents are looking for something different from what is currently broadly available in maintained primary schools.

Could parental choice change the face of maintained education?

The exercise of reflecting, however speculatively, on a different balance of availability which parents might ask for in educational provision leads us on to wonder whether parental choice might go further than to influence the teaching or organizational arrangements in certain schools, and actually change the whole face of maintained education as we know it. In other words, just how powerful might parental choice prove to be?

When the 1984 Green Paper 'Parental Influence at School' (DES, 1984) proposed a majority of parents on the governing bodies of maintained schools, it provoked strong reactions (Passmore, 1984). One opponent of the proposal spoke apprehensively of the possibility that an unpredictable giant of parental power, hitherto dormant, might be awakened and overwhelm the schools (Swallow, 1984). The Green Paper's proposal was not enacted.[10] Is it possible that 'opting out and open enrolment' might provide the reveille call for a sleeping giant?

I think not. Parental choice, the 'key element of government policy' as embodied in the 1988 Education Reform Act, is a considerable advance on the arrangements for choice enabled by the 1986 Act, but it is not a recipe for unfettered parental power. The voucher proposal, exchangeable for a place in any public or private school of the parents' choice, might have proved a recipe for such power, changing the face of education as we know it, and this is no doubt one of the reasons why the proposal has gone no further.[11]

This book began by asking whether parents were being used by government to bring about politically motivated changes in schools, or whether choosing their children's schools was something which parents had their own motivations for undertaking. Subsequent discussion has tried to show that parents are not wholly unprepared for the exercise of choice, and their choices will influence not only their own children's education but also, to some extent, the education of all children. But the 'political tool' aspect of parental choice must not be overlooked. It has not been stated that to down-grade the local government of education is a 'key element' of central government's policy, but the observer might conclude this to be so. The Education Reform Act has pre-empted the exercise of free parental choice by introducing two new forms of schooling (grant-maintained schools and city colleges) for which there is no clear-cut *a priori* evidence of parental demand. LEAs have no hand in these new forms of education, and their control over their existing educational domain is constrained by almost all the provisions of the Reform Act: the national curriculum, local management of schools and the 'open enrolment' aspect of parental choice. Power taken away from LEAs has not been and will not be handed over to unpredictable parents, however. Parental choice will not be a passport to parental power.

It has been Conservative policy, during the 1980s, which has put parental choice on the statute book. Might the policy of a future Labour government remove it? Such reversals are not easy. A policy to restrict or remove parental choice would not be an appealing item on any political manifesto, and the Labour Party has shown no propensity to oppose the presentation of parents as important actors on the educational scene. Rather, it has sought to show that the Conservative rhetoric on parental choice is hollow, and that parents are 'squashed' rather than empowered by the effects of the Reform Act.[12] Parental choice under a Labour government may be different, but it is sure to feature in some way on the political agenda.

There are those who claim to ignore the political connotations of education policy, and to be concerned only for 'the best interests of the children'. These apolitical professionals nevertheless have their apprehensions about the effects of parental choice. They fear that schools will feel pressured to market themselves in an unsuitably commercial way, and that giving weight to what parents want from schools will devalue professional educational judgements. To allay their fears, we conclude with a look at what may be some of the good effects of a policy for parental choice.

Beneficial long-term effects of a policy for parental choice

The potential strengths of a policy are often the reverse side of the coin from its weaknesses. New ideas or changes which can be perceived as disturbing and harmful by the professionals they will affect, also have the potential to provide beneficial long-term effects. Four main long-term beneficial effects of a policy for parental choice can be foreseen:

1 clearer aims for individual institutions;
2 greater respect for the client by professionals;
3 greater commitment by parents to schools their children attend;
4 livelier parental interest in education generally.

These points will be discussed in turn.

CLEARER AIMS FOR INDIVIDUAL INSTITUTIONS

The aims of some schools in the public sector have indeed been 'comprehensive', but this has sometimes been at the expense of clarity. 'To meet all the needs of all the pupils'[13] is more of a pious hope than an aim. It indicates a willingness to respond but not to define, initiate or guide. Schools whose pupils will join them as an outcome of parental choice rather than local authority allocative procedures will be motivated to spell out the kinds of needs which can appropriately be met by a school for a particular age group, and set out their resources and expertise for meeting those needs. Some schools will want to claim specialist skills, and will emphasize the suitability of the school for children with particular interests or inclinations. But clarity of aims is not just a matter of skilled brochure preparation. Parents who visit the school will want to find that the aims spelled out in writing are also on the lips of whoever receives them, and be shown some evidence that these same aims are the guide for school practice.

If a school is to have a *raison d'etre* which reveals itself to potential parents, to pupils and to the local community, then the headteacher, the governors and all the school staff need a common viewpoint on what the school stands for. Schools are in fact being encouraged, by various DES initiatives,[14] to prepare school development plans which, within a context of national and local aims, lay down a set of organizational and curricular targets, to be achieved over a specified time period. These plans should be jointly developed by 'headteachers and governors'.[15]

Management relations in schools, and school–governing body relations, are currently in the melting pot. Many groups are vying to provide training and guidance in these areas.[16] Whether or not heads, teachers and governors get access to the training they may feel they need, both the climate of parental choice and governmental pressure will spur them to clarify what their school has to offer to its potential clients.

GREATER RESPECT FOR THE CLIENT BY PROFESSIONALS

Apart from the need to make the school's identity and purpose clear to potential parents, schools in a climate of parental choice need to value the families whose children already attend the school.

I have indicated elsewhere (Johnson, 1989) that recent developments in education will lead schools to adopt a new attitude to home–school relations. The requirement to maintain an accurate list of parents and guardians of pupils at the school (Education Reform Act 1988, s. 60) means that schools must inform themselves more accurately about the identity of the parents with whom they share the task of educating the children on the school's roll.[17] In many schools it has not hitherto been thought important to keep a register of the parent body. Pupil post has been relied on for communication between school and home. Certain families are well known to the school, but in other cases, particularly in sizeable secondary schools, connections are not always made between family members in different years of the school. In schools where an accurate single list of parents' names and addresses does exist, it has usually been laboriously compiled by the parents' association, for fund-raising purposes. Identifying parents as individuals, rather than as the mother or father of a particular child, can be the first step towards appreciating that the parent has an individual point of view about the school, and a set of expectations about the school's role. Hirschman (1970) suggests three options are available to those faced with inadequacies in an organization with which they are involved. These options are Exit, Voice and Loyalty.[18] Parental choice of school implies not only an exercise of preference for a chosen school, but also the Exit option of withdrawal from a school that does not meet expectations.

Parents can be governors of the school, and school governing bodies have come out of obscurity to play a prominent part in each school's present and future. The 1986 Act gave parents equal representation with the local authority on the school's governing body, and the Reform Act gives governors a share in responsibility for many new aspects of school life, including the delivery of the national curriculum and the management of the school's finances.

Parents now have an increased number of representatives on a body with a new and important role. Recognizing parents as valid electors of a substantial section of the governing body means recognizing that not only Exit but Voice is available to them.

Some teachers are reluctant to recognize parents as clients of the school. The pupil is the client, they claim, but this is to ignore the legal position of minors in a society where education is compulsory to the age of sixteen. When they are dissatisfied, pupils do indeed exercise some of the options open to clients: the Exit option by truanting, or the Voice option by active expression of their disaffection.[19] In these circumstances, however, it is ultimately the parents with whom the school has to deal, and therefore the parents who are the professional teacher's legal clients. If the third option of Loyalty to the school is to be embraced, it must be embraced by parents as well as their children, and a policy of parental choice can play a part in this.

GREATER COMMITMENT BY PARENTS TO SCHOOLS THEIR CHILDREN ATTEND

Rumours of the impending closure of almost any school awaken emotional and active response from many of the parents of its pupils. The predictability of this defensive response suggests that there is a latent force of loyalty available in any parent body which becomes overt only when danger threatens.

Cynics may suggest that parents are only reacting to the threat that they will have to make new arrangements for the daytime care of their children, and do not actually value the school as a distinctive and irreplaceable institution. But even if loyalty is motivated largely by family convenience, this is a realistic basis. Schools *are* in contract with parents to care for their children during school hours. Parents who work, and who have had to pay for their children to be looked after during pre-school years, know the value to be placed on the custodial role of the school. Teachers sometimes feel that undue emphasis is placed on their custodial responsibilities for their pupils. Nevertheless they accept these responsibilities, and demonstrate this by giving parents due notice if the school will not be open for any reason, or seeking parental agreement if a child is to leave school earlier or later than usual on a particular day. But the role of a school as a place of safety is only one reason for the kind of parental commitment which comes to the surface when the continuance of a school is threatened.

Unless marked crises occur in home–school relations, families do tend to feel some loyalty to the schools their children attend on a daily basis over a number of years, but may feel under no obligation to demonstrate that loyalty. I have argued at length elsewhere (Johnson and Ransom, 1983; Johnson, 1990) that parents who have little to do with their children's schools are not necessarily apathetic about their education. Nevertheless, for teachers, a more obvious and active commitment by parents would be encouraging. There is every likelihood that a policy of parental choice which really works for parents, giving them places at the schools they select for their children, will enliven parental loyalty to the point where it shows. Maintained schools whose pupils are on roll as a matter of family preference rather than bureaucratic placement can hope for the kind of percentage response to school invitations, and backing for school undertakings, which many independent schools enjoy. A highly visible parent body, demonstrating some of the unexpected skills, and articulating some of the perhaps unanticipated expectations, which have hitherto been hidden, can of course be hard to handle. But schools which welcome their free-choice families as valued clients who understand what the school is trying to do, will be mobilizing a resource of loyalty and commitment which they may soon wonder how they ever did without.

LIVELIER PARENTAL INTEREST IN EDUCATION GENERALLY

In chapter 1, brief reference was made to Baron *et al.*'s (1981) thesis developed in *Unpopular Education*. These writers contend that the advent of institutionalized education, and compulsory schooling, put paid to any aspirations which the working class may have had to acquire Really Useful Knowledge.[20] Schooling simply became another way to keep the mass of people in their (disadvantaged) place in society. As a consequence, and despite much 're-forming' of education during the twentieth century, the majority of people in Britain have never come to value education, and the school years are seen as a time to be got through before real life can start.

Varying schools of thought offer competing analyses of the founding and development of publicly funded education in Britain, but there is a ring of truth in the assertion that education is not highly valued by most people in our society. Comparisons are hazardous – as like is rarely being compared with like – but the age at which compulsory schooling ends, the percentage of young people stopping on for extended schooling, the proportion undertaking any form of further or higher education, even the length of our degree courses, appear to indicate that the demand for education in Britain has not forced its supply up to the level which is common in other Western countries.[21]

To say that parental choice in education could change all this would be an exaggerated claim. But a policy for parental choice makes the assumption that the majority of people, for whom education has perhaps been an 'unpopular' service in the past, are ready for a change. Four or five generations of compulsory schooling, even if they have not roused enthusiasm for school, have given those of us who have relied on publicly maintained schools a history of involvement with educational institutions, a certain familiarity with the processes of teaching and learning, and, perhaps, an awareness of where there is room for improvement. The powerlessness of the schooled, and their families, in our public systems of education during the twentieth century has been remarkable. Parents have not strongly sought to change schools, but their dissatisfactions have sometimes led them to overlook their children's non-attendance, particularly in the final secondary years. Teachers too have sometimes concluded there is nothing to be gained from insisting on a pupil's attendance at classes he or she finds irrelevant. The practice of condoned non-attendance at many of our secondary schools during the 1970s (Bird *et al.*, 1981) has not been an unknown phenomenon in the 1980s.[22] But since 1986 the greater permeability of schools to outside influence has, with other developments,[23] brought education into the limelight and started to give parents the feeling that they can and should become more involved in the process of schooling and its outcomes.

Parents already are educators, perhaps the most effective educators that their children have, but they are not educationalists. Some parents will play a part in the tasks of school government, but they will not be taking over the running of schools from professionals, nor bringing about a transformation in curriculum and teaching methods. Nevertheless, and importantly, they will be contributing their approval, or disapproval, of what goes on in schools by the choices they make on behalf of their children. Parental choice as a policy may make education truly popular at last.

Notes

Chapter 1

1 BBC News at 6 p.m., 22 February 1989, when the first two schools received approval for grant-maintained status.
2 Stone (1979) provides useful source material on the functions of the pre-industrial family in Britain. See also Burnett (1982) for nineteenth-century material on the family and education.
3 In 1989 coordinated non-attendance at certain maintained schools was used by Muslim parents in a Midlands town to bring pressure to bear for the creation of single-sex schools. This boycotting action undoubtedly had political connotations, but its influence did not extend beyond the immediate locality.
4 Section 76 of the 1944 Education Act required LEAs to have regard to the general principle that children were to be educated in accordance with their parents' wishes in so far as this was compatible with the provision of efficient instruction and training and the avoidance of unreasonable public expenditure.
5 Parents may appeal to the secretary of state under Section 68 of the 1944 Act that the LEA (or school governors) have acted 'unreasonably'. Also, under section 37 of the 1944 Act parents against whom a school attendance order was served had to be given an opportunity to select the school their child should attend. This school had to be named in the order unless the Secretary of State otherwise directed under subsection (3). However, section 10 of the 1980 Education Act replaced arbitration by the Secretary of State under section 37(3) (for all except pupils in need of special educational treatment) by the opportunity to appeal to a local appeals committee (Meredith, 1981).
6 During 1977 the Secretary of State received 1,124 complaints under section 68 over secondary school allocations. All but 2 were rejected. In the same year LEAs applied to the secretary of state for directions under section 37(3) in respect of 40 children, and the school

determined was that preferred by the parent in 24 cases (Meredith, 1981, pp. 78–9).

7 Woods (1979, p. 136) in a brief discussion of paternalism states that: 'The two key elements in *pater's* position are (a) infallibly knowing what is good for those he governs, and (b) dispensing it in ways he chooses on the grounds of superior expertise.'

8 Section 5 of the 1976 Education Act gave the secretary of state powers to require LEAs to pay for private places only in accordance with regulations approved by the secretary of state, and to revoke previous arrangements (Salter and Tapper, 1985, p. 119).

9 Nearly all the Catholic direct grant schools joined the maintained sector when grants were phased out. Most of the other direct grant schools however became fully independent.

10 This brief account of stages in and responses to the equality argument is necessarily over-simplified. Useful additional sources are Kogan (1978, ch. 9) for a general analysis of developments to that date, Salter and Tapper (1985) on the case of the independent schools, Weiner and Arnot (1987) for references relevant to gender and equality in education.

11 League tables of expenditure on education and other public services are regularly published by the Chartered Institute of Public Finance and Accounting (CIPFA). See also Lord (1984).

12 It has been suggested that 'cultural capital' is what educated parents, knowledgeable about and in agreement with the cultural aims of formal education, bring to their involvement with schools. Bourdieu (1973) was the first proponent of this much quoted 'cultural capital' idea. See also Halsey, Heath and Ridge (1980) and Walford (1984).

13 In January 1988, and again in February 1989, a severe shortage of school places was reported in Tower Hamlets, East London. A report on primary education in the borough, prepared by ILEA, stated that as many as 400 children, mainly of Bangladeshi origin, had no school place in Tower Hamlets (*TES*, 22 January 1988). Despite an expansion of primary places, a year later there were reported to be some 500 children, mostly aged 6 and 7 years, unplaced in school (*TES*, 24 February 1989). A rapid increase in the local school age population and a teacher shortage in inner London combined to create a crisis, which was partly alleviated by the recruitment of teachers from West Germany, Denmark and the Netherlands (*TES*, 1 September 1989).

14 Halsey (1975) expresses disillusionment with the possibility of reaching an egalitarian society by educational reform. In his view the role of education can only be to maintain such a society once it has been attained by economic and political reform.

15 In this paragraph I have drawn on Coons and Sugarman's succinct discussion of the intellectual history of choice in education (Coons and Sugarman, 1978, pp. 18–19).

16 Section 36 of the Education Act (1944) states: 'It shall be the duty of the parent of every child of compulsory school age to cause him to receive efficient full-time education . . . either by regular attendance at school or otherwise'. Home-based education is discussed in chapter 2.

17 Illich (1971) advocates 'de-schooling' society, on the grounds that obligatory schools divide social reality into 'educational' schooling and 'non-educational' daily living.

18 'Public Choice' theorists contend that self-interest of the organization is at the heart of all negotiation within policy-making (Niskanen 1971; Borcherding 1977), so that budgets have an inbuilt tendency to expand.

19 There is a considerable literature on the accountability of schools and education systems, for example Becher and Maclure (1978), Sockett (1980), Lacey and Lawton (1981), McCormick (1982). It is summarized and debated by Kogan (1986).

20 Similar arguments about the rights of children are put forward by David (1978) from a Marxist-feminist perspective. Associated arguments about whether parents' rights over their children's education can be argued for on religious grounds are debated by McLaughlin (1984) who concludes that any form of 'indoctrination' through education may impede the autonomy of the child's personal and moral development.

21 For a full commentary on all sections of the Education Reform Act see Maclure (1988).

22 Responses to consultative documents about the 1988 Education Reform Act were not published by government but made available in *Take Care Mr. Baker!*, edited by Haviland (1988). Subsequent discussion here, with quotations from Haviland's compendium, is referenced by the name of the responding institution or individual, followed by the page reference in *Take Care Mr. Baker!* (TCMB).

23 The 'standard number' concept was introduced by the 1980 Education Act. At the time of writing the usual standard number is equivalent to the pupil intake of the school in question in 1979.

24 Some would dispute whether the spread was equitable in the years *before* the 1988 Act.

25 See, for example, the Open University's Course E325, Managing Schools (Open University, 1988).

26 Core subjects are mathematics, English and science, also Welsh for schools in Wales which are Welsh speaking. Foundation subjects are history, geography, technology, music, art, physical education, a modern foreign language for 11 to 16-year-olds and Welsh for schools in Wales which are not Welsh speaking. Together with religious education for all pupils, these core and foundation subjects comprise the 'basic curriculum' of maintained schools (1988 Education Reform Act, ss. 2 and 3).

27 Use of the words 'the same good and relevant curriculum' in the consultative document assumed a consensus on relevance (DES, 1987a, p. 4).

28 During 1988 and 1989 National Curriculum Subject Working Groups were preparing their reports for the secretary of state. These reports make recommendations about attainment targets and programmes of work for each of the foundation subjects, as 'the basis for consultation about what is eventually set out in regulations for the curriculum' (DES, 1987a, p. 6).

29 There are certain similarities between the former direct grant and the new grant-maintained schools, in particular their direct funding by the DES. However direct grant schools were independent secondary schools, the majority of whose pupils were fee-paying. As a condition of their grant they offered a percentage of free places to pupils from local authority primary schools, and reserved further fee-paying places for take-up by the LEA in which they were located. Grant-maintained schools, which may be primary or secondary, are state schools and are prohibited from charging fees. Their only obligation to the LEA is to provide them with annual statistics.

30 Schools are not however eligible for grant-maintained status if proposals by the LEA to cease to maintain the school have received necessary approval from the secretary of state or, in the case of a voluntary school, if governors have notified their intention to discontinue the school under section 13 of the 1944 Education Act (1988 Education Reform Act, ss. 52(8) and (9)).

31 At the consultation stage, several groups pressed for the stipulation of a particular percentage of parents in favour of grant-maintained status before an application could go forward. However, the Reform Act requires only a majority.

32 By October 1989, twenty-seven proposals had been approved by the secretary of state and five rejected, while proposals had been published for fourteen more schools.

33 Research by Kogan *et al.* (1984) showed that whatever their relative numbers, lay governors were less powerful than teaching professionals on the governing body. However, parents on the first governing bodies of grant-maintained schools are likely to be experienced campaigners on behalf of their school, so may be more effective than lay governors of other schools.

34 Skegness Grammar school, one of the first to be awarded grant-maintained status, emphasized that it would seek to augment its funds by sponsorships (*TES*, 24 February 1989). Subsequently, some county schools have followed a similar line.

35 Section 58(3) of the Reform Act makes this stipulation, but see also section 102 which allows for trust deeds to be modified following consultation.

36 Research into the progress of the first city technology colleges was

funded by the ESRC for 3 years from April 1988. The project, 'A new choice of school? An evaluation of the CTC initiative', is being directed from Bristol Polytechnic and Newcastle University.

37 Maclure (1988) takes the view that although not bound by the national curriculum, in practice CTCs are likely to meet all or most of its requirements. More long-established independent schools have also indicated their intention to take account of the national curriculum.

38 Brighouse (1989) suggests that LEAs will have to be very careful how they handle the schools in LMS negotiations, otherwise many of them may opt out.

Chapter 2

1 As noted in the preface, discussion in this book relates mainly to schools in England, although the research into parental choice of maintained schools discussed in chapter 3 also covers Scottish education. Education in Wales, Scotland and Northern Ireland differs in a number of ways from the English system.

Wales: Education Acts apply both to England and Wales except where specific provisions are made. For example, sections 227–29 of the 1988 Education Reform Act relate only to Wales. Most official circulars and regulations are issued jointly by the Welsh Office and the Department of Education and Science, but regulations may make different provision for Wales. Welsh education is chiefly distinguished by the existence of a number of Welsh-speaking schools, where English is a second language.

Scotland: In Scotland the Minister for Education, the Secretary of State for Scotland, acts through the Scottish Education Department in Edinburgh. Scotland has completely separate educational legislation, and in the past has differed considerably from the English system. However, recent legislation has brought the two systems closer together. For example, the 1981 Education Act in Scotland followed the 1980 Education Act in England and was drafted on similar lines (with certain exceptions which are discussed in chapter 3).

Northern Ireland: Northern Ireland also has its own Department of Education and separate legislation. Distinguishing features of the education system in Northern Ireland are its essentially selective nature, with 11 plus selection and a large number of grammar schools, and the prevalence of voluntary schools, most of which practise religious segregation of Catholics and Protestants.

Voluntary Grammar schools in Northern Ireland are known as 'Assisted' schools (as are 'Grant-Aided' schools in Scotland). These schools are 'administered and financed by governing bodies which have a substantial degree of autonomy but which receive a grant direct from central government sources. In Northern Ireland all Voluntary

Grammar schools (except for three) reserve at least 80% of the places available in each school year for the admission of non-fee-paying pupils to the secondary departments. Voluntary Grammar school pupils account for about 25% of all secondary school pupils in Northern Ireland' (Central Statistical Office, 1989, Notes on Education, n. 2).

Brief descriptive accounts of education in Scotland, Northern Ireland and Wales, by N. Grant, J. Fulton and R. Webster respectively, are to be found in Cohen, Thomas and Manion (1982). A more recent reference for Northern Ireland is Osborne, Cormack and Miller (1987).

2 In the case of voluntary aided schools, governors are responsible, under the 1944 Education Act (section 15(3) (a)), for certain types of alteration and repairs to the school buildings. The DES make a 'maintenance contribution' of eighty-five per cent of sums expended by the governors in respect of these obligations. The remaining fifteen per cent has to be found by the governors. This fifteen per cent obligation does not apply in voluntary controlled schools. See Brooksbank *et al.* (1985) for a more detailed discussion of the position of voluntary schools of all types.

3 The 1988 Education Reform Act has changed the position of the LEA in relation to schools which seek and obtain grant-maintained status. For voluntary schools the Diocesan Board or similar body has a potentially important role to play, although with some of their schools the relationship is a tenuous one.

4 The principal associations of which headteachers or schools may be in membership are: the Headmasters' Conference (HMC), of which a few headteachers of maintained schools are also members, the Incorporated Association of Preparatory Schools (IAPS), the Governing Bodies Association (GBA), the Girls' Schools Association (GSA), the Governing Bodies of Girls' Schools Association (GBGSA), the Society of Headmasters of Independent Schools (SHMIS) and the Independent Schools' Association Incorporated (ISAI). Other relevant organizations are the Independent Schools Joint Council (ISJC), the Secondary Heads' Association (SHA) and the Independent Schools Information Service (ISIS).

5 See note 2 above.

6 Personal communication from Professor Geoffrey Alderman.

7 DES Circular 2/89 makes it clear that LEAs and schools have discretion to charge for activities provided wholly or mainly outside school hours if these activities are optional extras, not required to meet the school's statutory curriculum obligations, or to complete the syllabus for a prescribed public examination. LEAs and schools must first draw up statements of their policies for charging, and say in what circumstances some parents might be exempt from charges. A summary of this information must be included in future prospectuses

published by the school. Parents may still be invited to make voluntary contributions to school funds or in support of any specific project. However, if an activity which is dependent on voluntary contributions for its survival goes ahead, it must be made clear that no pupil will be excluded because his or her parents have not contributed to the cost.

8 See Johnson (1987, ch. 1) for a discussion of key developments in the relationship between private schools and state schools.

9 Of the 531,500 pupils educated in non-maintained schools in England in 1988, 273,100 were at schools in the south-east. The remainder were distributed as follows: south-west 64,900; north-west 52,700; West Midlands 42,300; Yorkshire and Humberside 30,500; East Midlands 28,700; East Anglia 22,700; the north 16,500. In Wales 11,800 children were in non-maintained schools. Figures for Scotland and Northern Ireland, which include assisted schools, are 32,500 and 44,500 pupils respectively (Central Statistical Office, 1989, table 9.1).

10 Direct Grant Grammar Schools (Cessation of Grant) Regulations 1975, S.I. 1975/1198.

11 From time to time objections are raised over the unavailability of a fully secular education in England. (See for example Pateman (1988) and subsequent correspondence in the *Times Educational Supplement*, 4 March 1988 and 25 March 1988.) However, the call for secular education has not so far received popular support.

12 Remedial education by expert teachers of disadvantaged children receives federal funding in the USA under Title I of the Elementary and Secondary Education Act. Many of these teachers went into religious schools in the low-income inner-city areas. However the United States Supreme Court ruled (in two separate cases in 1985 and 1987) that the employment in parochial schools of teachers paid by the Federal Government was in violation of the First Amendment to the Constitution, which prohibits any link between church and state, and could not be permitted to continue.

13 This proviso about Christian worship does not apply to voluntary aided schools, some of which are of Jewish foundation.

14 Pupils at maintained special schools are excepted from this requirement.

15 The two societies were, respectively, The National Society for Promoting the Education of the Poor in the Principles of the Established Church (founded in 1811), and The British and Foreign School Society (1814).

16 The Catholic Poor Schools Committee received its first instalment of State financial aid in 1847.

17 This arrangement went through in the face of considerable opposition. 'Rome on the rates!' was one theme of resistance to rate aid for non-provided schools, many of which were Roman Catholic.

18 For example, in Church of England voluntary aided schools 'foundation' governors may be nominated by the Parochial Church Council, the Deanery Synod and the Diocesan Board.

19 'In all circumstances, the actual dismissal of a teacher in an aided school is by the governors' (Brooksbank *et al.*, 1985, p. 94, n. 151). However such dismissal must be with the consent or by the requirement of the LEA. A sole exception is under section 28(2) of the 1944 Education Act. Governors have the exclusive right to dismiss a teacher appointed by them to give religious instruction as required by the school's foundation, if the teacher has failed to give such instruction suitably and efficiently.

20 In *A Future in Partnership* (National Society, 1984, p. 98) it is stated that the twin aims of the Church of England in its schools are service to the nation and Christian education. *Faith in the City*, the report of the Archbishop of Canterbury's Commission on Urban Priority areas (1985), affirms that there are no hard and fast distinctions between church schools and local authority schools. 'Some Church schools are very like their neighbours. Christians can be involved in the management and teaching in both kinds of schools' (para 13.84).

21 An example was Headfield (Church of England controlled) Middle School, Kirklees LEA, where between eighty and ninety-three per cent of pupils were Asian. Parents' boycott of the school in 1987 became known as the 'Dewsbury affair'. The dispute is further discussed in chapter 6.

22 The Roman Catholic Church has only one controlled school, which failed to claim aided status within the required deadline (personal communication to the author).

23 The Sacred Heart High School in Hammersmith and Fulham. Entry criteria for 1990.

24 Statistics provided by the Methodist Church Division of Education and Youth show that by 1989 Methodist voluntary schools were slightly fewer than Table 2.1 indicates for 1987. In October 1989 there were 29 Methodist voluntary schools, of which 2 were aided. There were also 26 joint Anglican/Methodist schools (included in the 'Other' category of Table 2.1), of which 9 were aided. All the other schools were voluntary controlled. Joint Anglican/Methodist schools 'are founded to provide education in a Christian ambience, not just for the children of Anglican and the children of Methodist parents but for all children whose parents wish them to benefit from what the schools can give' (Joint Working Party, General Synod Board of Education and Methodist Division of Education and Youth, 1978).

25 See, for example, Wallace (1988).

26 Following HMI inspection and a notice of complaint, unless remedial action is taken by the proprietors, schools are struck off the Independent Schools Register. In 1985 several small 'Christ-centred' schools had notices of complaint served on them. The notices referred

to inadequately qualified staff and inadequate resources, but also highlighted curriculum deficiencies, in these cases of curriculum materials produced by Accelerated Christian Education of Louisville, Kentucky, USA. In another case, concerning the Talmud Torah Machzikei Hadass School of Clapton Common, London, the secretary of state in 1985 withdrew a notice of complaint following a tribunal hearing. HMI had, in 1983, criticized the school (which was provisionally registered pending transfer to full registration) on grounds of inadequate premises, but chiefly because of curriculum imbalance, with too short a time being given to secular education. Hebrew studies predominated. At the Independent Schools Tribunal hearing, counsel for the school established that the inspection team did not have the linguistic ability and knowledge of Hebrew studies and history to enable them to write a competent report. The notice of complaint was withdrawn without an order being made.

These cases illustrate the clash which sometimes occurs between the kind of education favoured by the community the school serves, and the minimum standards laid down by HMI for independent schools. They also show the wide range of skills required of HM Inspectorate.

27 The debate about the desirability of Muslim education within the maintained sector continues. In 1989, the Government view was that if Muslim schools were big enough to be viable and to offer the national curriculum, their application for voluntary aided status would be considered 'in the normal way'. The Labour party initially favoured giving Muslim parents the same rights as Anglicans, Catholics and Jews to have their own schools in the state system, but following dispute about whether Islamic schools offer equal opportunity to girls, the party's support for Muslim state schools has been muted (see Broom (1989) and Labour Party (1989)).

28 The Fleming Report applied this term only to certain boarding schools but it is often used to cover both boarding and day schools in membership of HMC. However the term 'public school' is confusing, and latterly has been replaced by reference to 'independent' schools. In this book the term public school is used only where unavoidable, as when referring to literature which uses the term.

29 The Fleming Committee suggested that boys and girls would 'learn from Boarding School life the habit of self dependence, of taking decisions and making plans without unnecessary reliance on the guidance or encouragement of their parents' (Board of Education, 1944, para 123).

30 Section 8 of the 1944 Act requires LEAs to have particular regard to the 'expediency of securing the provision of boarding education, either in boarding schools or otherwise, for pupils for whom education as boarders is considered by their parents and by the authority to be desirable'.

31 John Vaizey, then Professor of Economics at Brunel University, appended this Note of Reservation to the Report.

32 The Public Schools Commission noted noncommitally in 1968 that 'in the maintained secondary sector some 60 per cent of pupils are already in coeducational schools, and we do not know of any evidence that co-education is unsuccessful' (Public Schools Commission, 1968, para 302).

33 The annual guide prepared by ISIS, *Choosing your Independent School*, formerly listed schools as Preparatory, Boys' Senior, Girls' and Coeducational. Since 1987 schools have been categorized in the guide as Boys', Girls' or Coeducational, indicating the age range admitted by each school. The change seems to indicate a decreasing expectation that preparatory schools are for boys only.

34 One outcome of parental choice legislation in Scotland (research on which is discussed in chapter 3), has been an increase in appeals for under-age children to be given primary school places (Petch, 1987). However, the desirability of educating four year-olds in full-time primary classes is a matter of controversy.

35 In my interviews with parents who had used both public and private education for their children (Johnson, 1987), one mother was vehement that when discussing allegiance to independent schools or the state system, 'pre-school doesn't count!'.

36 For children who are not at school the 'compulsory' period of education ends with the sixteenth birthday. However, 'a pupil who attains the age of sixteen while a registered pupil, or who has been a registered pupil within the twelve months preceding his sixteenth birthday, does not reach the end of compulsory school age

(i) until the end of the appropriate Spring Term if he or she attains sixteen between 1st September and 31st January inclusively; or
(ii) until the Friday before the last Monday in May if s/he attains sixteen after 31st January but before 1st September'.

(Education Otherwise, 1985, p. 26)

37 Not only families but also companies and overseas schools are affiliated to WES. International schools that use English as the medium of education call on WES to provide curricula which are British rather than American based. WES also assists international schools by recruiting teachers to work abroad and organizing school inspections and school-based in-service training. It helps international companies set up nursery and primary schools for children of their staff overseas.

38 Diocesan bodies give advice to the governors of their voluntary schools about admissions, but are careful to refer to 'guidelines' rather than diocesan 'policy'. However, one effect of the 1988 Reform Act has been to call into question the scrupulous respect for governors' powers which has hitherto prevailed in the voluntary sector. In 1989,

governors of a Catholic aided secondary school wishing to 'opt out' from their LEA and become grant-maintained were frustrated by the refusal of their bishop to appoint the required number of governors so that this proposal could go forward. The bishop wished the school to become a sixth form college, and challenged the governors' right to oppose this policy change. This case is further discussed in chapter 5.

39 In the first six months of 1988 ISIS issued eleven press releases, with the following headlines: 'More pupils take up Assisted Places'; 'New summer schools guide published'; 'Biggest ever exhibition of independent schools'; 'Parents give boarding top marks'; 'Isis International launches new clearing house'; 'More pupils in independent schools'; 'New Assisted Places leaflet'; 'Updated guide meets special needs'; 'Independent schools' funding outstrips maintained threefold'; 'School fees at top of household budgets'; 'More pupils for independent schools'.

40 In the financial year 1988/9, the total cost to the Exchequer of the army, navy and air force boarding school allowances was £108.4 million, and for the diplomatic services £6.3 million.

41 The ceilings for diplomatic boarding school allowance are based on information obtained direct from over 150 schools which are members of the Headmasters' Conference, as recommended by the report of the Committee on Representational Services Overseas, 1963 (Cmnd 2276).

42 As explained in the preface, discussion in this book does not cover the education of children with special educational needs. A useful recent reference is Goacher *et al.* (1988).

43 £3.7 million in the financial year 1988/89.

44 The two (voluntary aided) maintained schools which operate as choir schools (Kings School, Peterborough and the Minster School, Southwell, Notts) are an exception to this rule. However, the other 35 choir schools attached to cathedrals are all independent.

45 However, LEAs occasionally give assistance with school fees on an *ad hoc* basis, for example if a child is already a pupil at a fee-paying school but the family has now fallen on hard times. In the latter case local authority help with fees is sought on the grounds of ensuring continuity of education for the child (Johnson, 1987, p. 24).

Chapter 3

1 Secretary of State for Education, 22 February 1989 (see chapter 1).

2 This particular recommendation does not appear in the discussion of the Plowden Committee's principal proposals, nor in their list of 'other proposals which deserve to be singled out'. However, it is one of 197 'main' recommendations, reiterated at the end of the Report (Central Advisory Council, 1967, vol. 1, p. 464).

3 Elliott's questionnaire, based on ideas gleaned from previous parent interviews, was a complex one, requiring parents to respond to 26 possible reasons and 17 possible sources of influence, and to give a rating to the relative importance of these. The questionnaire had to be completed during the 'coffee break' of the meeting. Elliott himself states: 'I would not claim that the questionnaire provides a basis for valid generalisation. At best it is indicative of general tendencies and trends' (Elliott *et al.*, 1981, vol. I, p. (d)).
4 The Schools, Parents and Social Services Project, 1974–77, conducted by the Educational Studies Unit, Department of Government, Brunel University. The research with schools and agencies is discussed in Johnson *et al.* (1980). For a full account of the research with parents see Johnson and Ransom (1983).
5 With Elizabeth Ransom and myself, Katherine Bowden interviewed some of the parents whose views are discussed in Johnson and Ransom (1983).
6 How the interviews were obtained and conducted is fully described in the Appendix to *Family and School* (Johnson and Ransom, 1983).
7 There were no first or middle schools in these boroughs at the time of the research.
8 The Edinburgh study of the origins, implementation and operation of section 1 of the Education (Scotland) Act 1981, funded by the ESRC from 1983 to 1985, was directed by Michael Adler of the Department of Social Policy and Social Work, University of Edinburgh. The Glasgow study of parental choice, funded by the Scottish Education Department from 1982 to 1985, was directed by Alastair Macbeth of the Department of Education, University of Glasgow. The NFER Information for Parental Choice project, funded by the National Foundation for Educational Research from 1983 to 1985, was directed by Andy Stillman of NFER.
9 See note 1, chapter 1.
10 This summary cannot however pre-empt the findings of Adler *et al.*'s 1989 publication, not available at the time of writing.
11 In the early 1980s, school councils were the nearest equivalent in the Scottish system to school governing bodies in England. For research into the operation of these councils see Macbeth, MacKenzie and Breckenridge (1980).
12 A sheriff in Scotland is roughly the equivalent of a high court judge in England. Solicitor's fees incurred by parents who make an appeal to the sheriff and do not receive legal aid were estimated in 1986 at over £400. If the appeal is unsuccessful, the parents have to meet their own costs. The Glasgow research team also point out that 'this matter of cost represents an element of inequity in the system; since it favours those who are either wealthy, self-sacrificial, or receive Legal Aid, those between are at a potential disadvantage' (University of Glasgow, 1986, p. 76).

13 These differences between the Edinburgh and Glasgow studies were by agreement. 'Although both studies would include surveys of parents, the Edinburgh groups would concentrate more upon national and regional political facets related to the legislation; upon socio-legal effects, especially concerned with appeals and Sheriff Court decisions; and upon patterns of movements between school. The Glasgow study . . . would focus more on the effects upon schools and families, upon reasons for choice and information and upon educational practice and concepts.' (University of Glasgow, 1986, p. 3).
14 Over thirty slightly different questionnaires were prepared for different categories of parents. This made the exercise simpler for parents (if accurately distributed), but more complicated for the researchers.
15 The report states without further comment that 'In the category "Other reasons" that of joining a sibling already at a school was the most frequently mentioned, appearing as 8.3% of all reasons given' (University of Glasgow, 1986, p. 308).
16 A subsequent work by Macbeth, director of the Glasgow study, brings together much of his thinking on the potential of the relationship between parents and school (Macbeth, 1989).
17 Pseudonyms were used to distinguish the four authorities.
18 Considerable pilot work was undertaken before the questionnaire was issued, ensuring that 'relevant' questions were asked. The researchers attribute the high response rate they achieved at least in part to the relevance of the questions (Stillman and Maychell, 1986, p. 77).

Chapter 4

1 The area of study comprised two adjoining local education authorities in the south-east of England: one a county, the other a metropolitan borough. In my account of the study (Johnson, 1987) I used the pseudonyms 'Morrowshire' and 'Robart'.
2 'Magnet' schools in the USA are enriched 'model' schools in deprived urban centres, drawing their intake from beyond their neighbourhood areas and offering an ambitious curriculum. Some concentrate on the sciences, others on the humanities, performing arts or business courses. Despite over-subscription these magnet schools try to avoid becoming wholly selective by taking pupils on a first-come, first-registered, basis, or by reserving a quota for those below average ability (Binyon, 1987). In April 1990, when the Inner London Education Authority's education responsibilities pass to London boroughs, Wandsworth proposes to introduce a magnet programme in its secondary schools, with a view to attracting back the thirty-five

per cent of pupils who either go to private schools or to schools outside Wandsworth (Blackburne, 1989). In July 1989 Bradford announced similar proposals.

3 Direct grant schools were also funded by government, but had many other characteristics not shared by grant-maintained schools (see note 29 in chapter 1).

4 Because of independent schools' individual admission policies, and the generally buoyant market for private education in the 1980s, getting a child into a school was never simply a question of writing a cheque. But parents did not feel as impotent or frustrated as when faced with procedures for choice in the maintained sector. Frequently they had found a maintained school they wanted, but had been unable to arrange for their child to attend it.

5 Nevertheless, the move of one child from maintained to private education sometimes had a 'domino' effect on the school careers of other children in the family. Parents were concerned to be financially 'fair' to all their children, and concluded that what was spent on one child should also be spent on the others (Johnson, 1987, ch. 9).

6 A judgement sample is one which is selected to reflect certain criteria in which the researcher is interested. It cannot be the basis for predictions on the basis of probability. A random sample, where all eligible persons have an equal chance of being selected for the sample, is needed if statistical generalizations are to be made.

7 Other more small-scale research on Assisted Places is reported by Douse (1985), Wall (1986) and Walford (1988). See also Tapper and Salter (1986) for a critical discussion of the Assisted Places policy.

8 On the subject of attitudes which parents hope traditional boys' independent schools will impart to their sons, see also Heward (1988). This study is based on letters from parents to an independent school head.

Chapter 5

1 Despite the numerous associations to which independent schools may be affiliated (see chapter 2, note 4), these schools retain a strong sense of individuality in their dealings with one another. Any links they establish with maintained schools tend to be even more individualized and *ad hoc*. Some examples are discussed in Johnson (1987).

2 For example, the independent schools are not required to teach the national curriculum, though may have declared their intention to use it as a guideline.

3 Maclure (1988, p. 27) points out that the standard number can be *increased* without reference to the secretary of state, where the proposal to do so is not contested (1988 Education Reform Act, s. 26(7)), but if the proposed increase is opposed it must go to the

secretary of state for a ruling. Any proposal to *decrease* the standard number would require an order from the secretary of state. The procedure for making and dealing with such an application is similar to the procedure for dealing with a change in a school's character or use. It entails the publication of notices and the consideration of objections. Moreover the only grounds on which the secretary of state can make the requested order is by having regard to any reduction in the school's capacity 'as compared with its capacity when the standard number was fixed – if for example accommodation has been taken out of use' (Maclure, 1988, p. 28).

4 By mid-October 1989, 19 ballots of parents regarding grant-maintained status had resulted in a 'no' vote. One of these (a girls' school) had been facing the loss of its single-sex status, until the authority decided to withdraw its reorganization plan. Other authorities have also decided to withdraw their secondary reorganization proposals to discourage further opting-out. In all, forty-eight ballots had received a 'yes' vote but proposals following five of these ballots had so far been rejected by the secretary of state. (Statistics from the Grant Maintained Schools Trust, 19/10/89.) One of the rejected schools received its majority 'yes' vote only in a second ballot, with a relatively small number of parents voting. (A second ballot is required if less than half of those eligible to vote do so first time. The second ballot is conclusive, regardless of turnout.)

5 Schools which have, by October 1989, been accorded grant-maintained status include schools that are already highly selective in their intake and others that are straightforwardly comprehensive. There are also a number of single-sex schools. Grammar schools are disproportionately represented in the first lists of grant-maintained schools, but in Buckinghamshire in 1989 an (aborted) proposal by the LEA to create a new local authority grammar school influenced the decision of certain comprehensive schools to ballot on the subject of grant-maintained status, as a way of *retaining* their comprehensive character. The result of the ballot is not available at the time of writing.

6 Parents whose child has an Assisted Place receive a bill for fees from which the government's agreed contribution has been deducted. This is paid directly to the school (Johnson, 1987, p. 65).

7 Section 17 of the 1980 Education Act describes the purpose of the Assisted Places scheme as 'enabling pupils who might otherwise not be able to do so to benefit from education at independent schools'.

8 Hart (1988, p. 169), points out that the Education Reform Bill granted 182 powers to the secretary of state (to 'make a ruling', 'approve' etc).

9 Appeal decisions in England differ from those in Scotland in that the additional level of appeal to the sheriff is not available.

10 During the first wave of grant-maintained applications some teaching staff declined the opportunity to transfer to employment at a grant-

maintained school, especially where the LEA had undertaken to offer alternative employment.

11 See Maclure (1988, p. 123) for a short discussion of the role of the Education Assets Board.

12 One of the schools given grant-maintained status from September 1989 was a middle school (deemed secondary), which opted out in an area where the local authority had planned to switch to junior schools and 11–16 comprehensives.

13 The elimination of sixth forms is a particularly touchy aspect of secondary reorganization. It is reported (Sutcliffe, 1989) that Walsall Borough Council, producer of the first local authority plan 'specifically designed to take account of open enrolment and local management policies', proposes the closure of three schools but has shelved the reorganization of uneconomic sixth forms to avoid the risk of the schools in question opting out of council control.

14 The General Synod is the principal council of the Church of England, and is made up of over 500 representatives of laity and clergy. The proposed Diocesan Boards of Education Measure seeks to update the 1955 Diocesan Education Committees Measure. Its intention is to bring about some strengthening of the diocesan position, which is largely advisory.

15 In my study of families using both public and private education, a boy who was not 'seriously scholastic, and did not spend his leisure time in mind-expanding pursuits' was not felt by his parents to need the 'intellectually encouraging environment' of an independent school, whereas his more cerebral brother did (Johnson, 1987, p. 109).

16 The question of whether parental choice will be influential enough to change the type of school provision in a locality is discussed in chapter 6.

17 At the time of writing there is little experience of the actual operation of city technology colleges, although eleven have announced opening dates for 1990 and 1991. Two opened in September 1989, and one in the previous year. The research into city technology colleges commissioned by the ESRC in 1988 (see chapter 1, note 36) has not yet been embarked upon.

Chapter 6

1 Jewish voluntary schools are only a small minority (see chapter 2, table 2.1).

2 Speech by Cardinal Hume to the National Conference of Priests, reported by Clifford Longley, Religious Affairs Editor of *The Times*, 6 September 1989.

3 Parents who refused to accept places for their children at Headfield school were reported to have done so not only on the grounds that the school provided insufficient Christian education, but also because

the school was not their first choice. They claimed there were vacant classrooms at schools they would have preferred, and that the council, in directing them to Headfield, was contravening the Race Relations Act by setting artificial limits at other schools in order to change the racial mix at Headfield. In addition they contended their children's development would suffer at Headfield because most pupils spoke English as a second language. The parents maintained throughout the dispute that their objections were cultural and not racially motivated.

4 The Swann Report on the Education of Children from Ethnic Minority Groups (1985) considered that such separation would not be desirable.

5 The 'Muslim Pupils in British Schools' project, funded by the ESRC and undertaken by the University of Cambridge Department of Education in association with the Islamic Academy, Cambridge, will report in 1990.

6 Walford (1986) found that the lack of senior female role models in mainly boys' schools was a disadvantage for girls in these schools.

7 Free secondary education in the maintained sector was only available on a 'scholarship' basis from 1906 until 1944. Following the 1944 Education Act, 'secondary education for all' was provided largely on a tripartite basis until about 1965.

8 This is not to say that other non-selective schools are uninterested in the academic standards their pupils achieve, merely that their interest is less visible to the outside world.

9 Only secondary schools, and one middle school, deemed secondary, have so far applied for grant-maintained status (as of October 1989).

10 The 1986 Education Act required each school governing body to have an equal number of parent governors and LEA-nominated governors.

11 Seldon (1986) contends that interests within the Department of Education and Science were the most effective opponents of the voucher idea.

12 Jack Straw, MP for Blackburn and Labour spokesman on education, writing of 'Parents squashed by the Tory steamroller', claims that freedom of choice envisaged by the Reform Act has proved an educational mirage (Straw, 1989).

13 The published aim of a comprehensive school in outer London, in the 1970s.

14 The DES' LEA Training Grant Scheme, DES Circular 7/88 on Local Management of Schools, and DES Circular 382/89 on Performance Indicators.

15 The Minister of State for Education, Angela Rumbold, in a speech to the Industrial Society Conference, 5/12/89, emphasized the need for a clear view of the purposes and functioning of any school or college, and said that it was for headteachers and governing bodies to draw up their school's development plan, to which performance indicators could then be applied.

16 Harrison (1989) lists courses on school management offered by the Industrial Society, the British Institute of Management, the Careers Research and Advisory Centre, Understanding British Industry, NAHT Management Development Services, the Secondary Heads Association, NFER Enterprises, the East Midland Five In-service Training Initiative and the School Management South Consortium. The National Association of Governors and Managers, the Open University and the Cooperative Union are among those who offer courses for school governors.

17 Because of the prevalence of divorce and re-marriage, many children whose parents share their custody have two homes and a different family name from that of one parent.

18 For further discussion of these concepts in the context of education see Johnson (1987) and Johnson *et al.* (1988).

19 Some schools channel the 'voice' of pupils through School Councils and similar semi-democratic bodies, but the relative powerlessness of the school pupil of compulsory school age means that these councils are more training grounds for democratic procedures than arenas of influence (Bird *et al.*, 1981).

20 For a discussion of this concept, see R. Johnson (1979).

21 The Institute of Manpower Studies (1989) reports that in 1984 only just over 50 per cent of 16-year-olds stayed on in education in Britain. Comparable percentages abroad were more than 90 per cent in Holland and Denmark, 85 per cent in Belgium and more than 60 per cent in West Germany. In higher education in Britain, working class students take up only 20 per cent of student places, although the classes from which they are drawn represent 58 per cent of the population.

22 No recent large-scale investigation of truancy has been mounted. Stoll and O'Keeffe's (1989) discussion of truancy in nine maintained secondary schools, although polemical in its thrust, is of interest in examining the concept of post-registration truancy and the extent to which parents and teachers turn a blind eye to children's non-attendance.

23 The Great Debate of the 1970s stimulated new discussion on public education. Along with legislation, the teachers' pay dispute kept education in the public eye during the mid to late 1980s.

Guide to reading

Parental choice of school is an issue which has hitherto chiefly been discussed by those firmly convinced of its value or those who oppose it. J. Coons and S. Sugarman's (1978) *Education by Choice* (Berkeley, Calif.: University of California Press) gives the historical background to ideas about parental choice of school in England and the USA, and provides a strong argument for the exercise of parental choice in the present day. The opposing view, that local authorities are best fitted to take an overall view of the allocation of pupils to schools, is well expressed by S. Ranson (1990) *The Politics of Reorganizing Schools* (London: Unwin Hyman), another volume in this series of *Key Issues in Education*.

A policy of parental choice has as one of its aims the improvement of schools in response to consumer preferences. A cogent and non-polemical analysis of how consumers can make their views known to organizations is given by A. Hirschman (1970) *Exit, Voice and Loyalty* (Cambridge, Mass.: Harvard University Press).

Recent research into how parents choose schools, how local authorities respond to parental choice, and how both maintained and independent schools adapt to a climate of competition is discussed in chapters 3 and 4 of this book. Full accounts of some of the relevant research are to be found in M. Adler, A. Petch and J. Tweedie's (1989) *Parental Choice and Educational Policy* (Edinburgh: Edinburgh University Press); T. Edwards, J. Fitz and G. Whitty's (1989) *The State and Private Education: an Evaluation of the Assisted Places Scheme* (London: Falmer); D. Johnson's (1987) *Private Schools and State Schools: Two Systems or One?* (Milton Keynes: Open University Press) and A. Stillman and K. Maychell's (1986) *Choosing Schools: Parents, LEAs and the 1980 Education Act* (Windsor: NFER-Nelson).

Government's education policy in the 1980s has been controversial and radical in its initiatives. The contributions made by various interest groups to the debate which preceded the passing of the 1988 Education Reform Act are usefully recorded by J. Haviland (1988) *Take Care Mr. Baker!*

(London: Fourth Estate). The Act itself is well analysed and explained in S. Maclure's (1988) *Education Re-formed* (London: Hodder and Stoughton).

References

Adler, M. E. and Raab, G. M. (1988), 'Exit, choice and loyalty: the impact of parental choice on admissions to secondary schools in Edinburgh and Dundee', *Journal of Education Policy*, vol. 3, no. 2, pp. 155–79.

Adler, M. E. and Tweedie, J. (1986), 'Parental choice: liberty or licence?', *Journal of the Law Society of Scotland*, August, pp. 305–10.

Adler, M. E., Petch, A. J. and Tweedie, J. W. (1987), 'The origins and impact of the parents' charter', in D. McCrone (ed.), *The Scottish Government Yearbook 1987* (Edinburgh: Unit for the Study of Government in Scotland, Edinburgh University), pp. 289–330.

Adler, M. E., Petch, A. J. and Tweedie, J. W. (1987a), 'When sheriffs differ', *Times Educational Supplement* (Scotland), 27 February.

Adler, M. E., Petch, A. J. and Tweedie, J. W. (1989), *Parental Choice and Educational Policy* (Edinburgh: Edinburgh University Press).

Archbishop of Canterbury's Commission on Urban Priority Areas (1985), *Faith in the City* (London: Church House Publishing).

Assisted Places Committee (1988), *Survey* (London: Assisted Places Committee).

Banks, O. (1955), *Parity and Prestige in English Secondary Education* (London: Routledge).

Bantock, G. H. (1969), 'Discovery methods' in C. B. Cox and A. G. Dyson (eds), *Black Paper Two: The Crisis in Education* (London: Critical Quarterly Society), pp. 110–18.

Baron, S., Finn, D., Grant, N., Green, M. and Johnson, R. (1981), *Unpopular Education* (London: Hutchinson).

Bastiani, J. (ed.) (1988), *Parents and Teachers 2* (Windsor: NFER-Nelson).

Becher, T. and Maclure, S. (eds) (1978), *Accountability in Education* (Slough: NFER).

Bennett, N. (1976), *Teaching Styles and Pupil Progress* (London: Open Books).

Binyon, L. (1987), 'Educational choice used to be regarded as heretical. Now it is the conventional wisdom', *The Times*, 9 September.
Bird, C., Chessum, R., Furlong, J. and (ed.) Johnson, D. (1981), *Disaffected Pupils* (Uxbridge: Department of Government, Brunel University).
Blackburne, L. (1989), 'Wandsworth magnets to attract £10 million investment', *Times Educational Supplement*, 16 June.
Board of Education (Public Schools Committee) (1944), *The Public Schools and the General Education System*, Fleming Report (London: HMSO).
Bone, A. (1983), *Girls and Girls-Only Schools: a review of the evidence* (Manchester: Equal Opportunities Commission).
Borcherding, T. E. (ed.) (1977), *Budgets and Bureaucrats: the Sources of Government Growth* (Durham, NC: Duke University Press).
Bourdieu, P. (1973), 'Cultural reproduction and social reproduction', in R. Brown (ed.), *Knowledge, Education and Cultural Change* (London: Tavistock), pp. 71–112.
Brighouse, T. (1989), 'Dodgy cocktails', *Times Educational Supplement*, 23 June.
Brooksbank, K., Revell, J., Ackstine, E. and Bailey, K. (1985), *County and Voluntary Schools* (Harlow: Councils and Educational Press).
Broom, D. (1989), 'Clash of fundamental freedoms', *The Times*, 24 July.
Burnett, J. (1982), *Destiny Obscure: Autobiographies of Childhood, Education and Family from the 1820s to the 1920s* (London: Allen Lane).
Bush, T. and Kogan, M. (1982), *Directors of Education* (London: Allen & Unwin).

Central Advisory Council for Education, England (1967), *Children and their Primary Schools*, Plowden Report, 2 vols (London: HMSO).
Central Statistical Office (1989), *Regional Trends 24* (London: HMSO).
Chanan, G. (1970), *Streaming and the primary teacher* (Slough: NFER).
Cohen, L., Thomas, J. and Manion, L. (eds) (1982), *Educational Research and Development in Britain 1970–1980* (Windsor: NFER-Nelson).
Coleman, J. (1978), 'Foreword', in J. E. Coons and S. D. Sugarman, *Education by Choice* (Berkeley, Calif.: University of California Press), pp. xi–xiv.
Committee of Enquiry into the Education of Children from Ethnic Minority Groups (1985), *Education for All*, Swann Report (London: HMSO).
Congregation for Catholic Education (1988), *The Religious Dimension of Education in a Catholic School* (London: Catholic Truth Society).
Coons, J. E. and Sugarman, S. D. (1978), *Education by Choice* (Berkeley, Calif.: University of California Press).
Crosland, C. A. R. (1964), *The Future of Socialism* (London: Jonathan Cape).
Cunningham, R. F. (1987), 'The Catholic school system in England and

Wales', Internal memorandum (London: Catholic Education Council). (Copies available from the Council.)

David, M. (1978), 'The family-education couple', in G. Littlejohn *et al.* (eds), *Power and the State* (London: Croom Helm), pp. 158–95.

Davis, A. (1950), *Social Class Influence on Learning* (Chicago: University of Chicago Press).

Deem, R. (ed.) (1984), *Co-education Reconsidered* (Milton Keynes: Open University Press).

Dennison, S. R. (1984), *Choice in Education* (London: Institute of Economic Affairs).

Dennison, W. (1989), 'Count your blessings', *Times Educational Supplement*, 6 October.

DES (1984), *Parental Influence at School* Cmnd 9242 (London: HMSO).

DES (1987), *Grant Maintained Schools: consultation paper* (London: DES).

DES (1987a), *The National Curriculum 5–16: a consultation document* (London: DES).

DES (1988), *Admission of pupils to county and voluntary schools* Draft Circular 11/88 (London: HMSO, 20 October).

Douglas, J. W. B. (1964), *The Home and the School* (London: MacGibbon and Kee).

Douse, M. (1985), 'The background of Assisted Places scheme students', *Educational Studies*, vol. 11, no. 3, pp. 211–17.

Duncan, G. (1989), 'A clash of perspective', *Times Educational Supplement*, 18 August.

Education Otherwise (1985), *School is Not Compulsory. A guide to home-based education* (Cambridge: Education Otherwise).

Edwards, T., Fitz, J. and Whitty, G. (1989), *The State and Private Education: an evaluation of the Assisted Places scheme* (London: Falmer).

Elliott, J. (1981), *Uplands. A school in the market place*, Vol. I in Elliott *et al.* (1981), *Case Studies in School Accountability*. (Cambridge: Cambridge Institute of Education).

Elliott, J. (1981a), 'How do parents judge schools?' in J. Elliott *et al.* (1981), *School Accountability* (London: Grant McIntyre), pp. 40–57.

Elliott, J., Bridges, D., Ebbutt, D., Gibson, R. and Nias, J. (1981), *Case Studies in School Accountability*, 3 vols (Cambridge: Cambridge Institute of Education).

Fitzherbert, L. and Eastwood, M. (eds) (1988), *The Educational Grants Directory* (London: Directory of Social Change).

Flew, A. (1983), *Power to the People!* (London Centre for Policy Studies).

Floud, J. (1961), 'Social class factors in educational achievement', in A. H. Halsey (ed.), *Ability and Educational Opportunity* (Paris: OECD), pp. 91–109.

Fox, I. (1984), 'The demand for a public school education: a crisis of confidence in comprehensive schooling', in G. Walford (ed.), *British Public Schools: policy and practice* (London: Falmer), pp. 45–63.
Fox, I. (1985), *Private Schools and Public Issues* (London: Macmillan).
Fraser, E. (1959), *Home Environment and the School* (London: University of London Press).
Friedman, M. (1962), *Capitalism and Freedom* (Chicago: University of Chicago Press).
Fulton, J. (1982), 'Education in Northern Ireland', in Cohen, Thomas and Manion, op. cit., pp. 227–40.

Gay, B. M. (1985), *The Church of England and the Independent Schools* (Abingdon: Culham Educational Foundation).
Glennerster, H. and Pryke, R. (1964), *The Public Schools* Young Fabian pamphlet (London: The Fabian Society).
Glennerster, H. and Wilson, G. (1970), *Paying for Private Schools* (London: Allen Lane).
Goacher, B., Evans, J., Welton, J. and Wedell, K. (1988), *Policy and Provision for Special Educational Needs* (London: Cassell Educational).
Gosden, P. H. J. H. (1983), *The Education system Since 1944* (Oxford: Martin Robertson).
Grant, N. (1982), 'Education in Scotland', in Cohen, Thomas and Manion, op. cit., pp. 215–26.
Gray, J. (1981), 'Are examination results a suitable measure of school performance?' in I. Plewis, J. Gray, K. Fogelman and P. Mortimore, *Publishing School Examination Results: a Discussion*, Bedford Way Papers 5 (London: University of London Institute of Education), pp. 13–23.
Gray, J., McPherson, A. F. and Raffe, D. (1983), *Reconstructions of Secondary Education* (London: Routledge).
Greenall, J. (1988), 'How to improve your image', *Times Educational Supplement*, 15 January.

Hall, V., Mackay, H. and Morgan, C. (1986), *Headteachers at Work* (Milton Keynes: Open University Press).
Halsey, A. H. (1975), 'Sociology and the equality debate', *Oxford Review of Education*, vol. 1, no. 1, pp. 9–23.
Halsey, A. H., Heath, A. F. and Ridge, J. M. (1980), *Origins and Destinations* (Oxford: Clarendon Press).
Halsey, A. H., Heath, A. F. and Ridge, J. M. (1984), 'The political arithmetic of public schools', in G. Walford (ed.), *British Public Schools: policy and practice*, pp. 9–44.
Harrison, P. (1989), 'Manageable menu', *Times Educational Supplement*, 29 September.
Hart, D. (1988), 'Who'll pay to prop the school gates open?' in J. Haviland (ed.), *Take Care Mr. Baker!* (London: Fourth Estate), pp. 168–70.

Haviland, J. (ed.) (1988), *Take Care Mr. Baker!* (London: Fourth Estate).
Heward, C. (1988), *Making a Man of Him: parents and their sons' education at an English public school, 1929–50* (London: Routledge).
Hillgate Group (1986), *Whose Schools?* (London: The Hillgate Group).
Hirschman, A. O. (1970), *Exit, Voice and Loyalty* (Cambridge, Mass.: Harvard University Press).
Honey, J. F. de S. (1977), *Tom Brown's Universe* (London: Millington).

Illich, I. (1971), *Deschooling Society* (London: Calder and Boyars).
Institute of Manpower Studies (1989), *How many graduates in the 21st century? The choice is yours* (Sussex: IMS, University of Sussex).
ISIS (1987), *Choosing Your Independent School* (London: ISIS).

Jackson, B. (1964), *Streaming: an education system in miniature* (London: Routledge).
Johnson, D. (1987), *Private Schools and State Schools: two systems or one?* (Milton Keynes: Open University Press).
Johnson, D. (1989), 'What's new in home–school relations?', *Management in Education*, vol. 2, no. 4, pp. 19–20.
Johnson, D. (1990), 'Parents, students and teachers: a three-way relationship', *International Journal of Educational Research* (forthcoming).
Johnson, D. and Ransom, E. (1980), 'Parents' perceptions of secondary schools', in M. Craft, J. Raynor and L. Cohen (eds), *Linking Home and School* (London: Harper & Row), pp. 177–85.
Johnson, D. and Ransom, E. (1983), *Family and School* (London: Croom Helm).
Johnson, D., Whitaker, T. and Kay, W. (1988), 'The external relations of schools', Block 6 of Open University Course E325 *Managing Schools* (Milton Keynes: Open University Press).
Johnson, D., Ransom, E., Packwood, T., Bowden, K. and Kogan, M. (1980), *Secondary Schools and the Welfare Network* (London: Allen & Unwin).
Johnson, R. (1979), ' "Really useful knowledge": radical education and working-class culture 1790–1848' in J. Clarke *et al.* (eds), *Working Class Culture* (London: Hutchinson), pp. 75–102.
Joint Working Party, General Synod Board of Education and Methodist Division of Youth (1978), *Joint Anglican/Methodist Schools* (London: General Synod Board of Education and Methodist Division of Youth).

Kogan, M. (1978), *The Politics of Educational Change* (London: Fontana).
Kogan, M. (1986), *Education Accountability* (London: Hutchinson).
Kogan, M., Johnson, D., Packwood, T. and Whitaker, T. (1984), *School Governing Bodies* (London: Heinemann).

Labour Party (1985), *Labour's Charter for Pupils and Parents* (London: Labour Party).

Labour Party (1989), *Multi-cultural Education, Labour's Policy for Schools* (London: Labour Party).
Lacey, C. and Lawton, D. (1981), *Issues in Evaluation and Accountability* (London: Methuen).
Lambert, R. (1975), *The Chance of a Lifetime?* (London: Weidenfeld and Nicolson).
Leinster-Mackay, D. (1984), *The Rise of the English Prep School* (London: Falmer).
Limerick, B. (1989), 'Busybodies, antibodies and nobodies – a study of community involvement in secondary schools'. Paper presented to the Research Group, Department of Social and Educational Studies, University of British Columbia. Unpublished.
Lord, R. (1984), *Value for Money in Education* (London: Public Money).
Lunn, J. C. Barker (1970), *Streaming in the primary school: a longitudinal study of children in streamed and non-streamed junior schools* (Slough: NFER).

Macbeth, A. (1989), *Involving Parents* (Oxford: Heinemann).
Macbeth, A., MacKenzie, M. and Breckenridge, I. (1980), *Scottish School Councils: policy-making, participation or irrelevance?* (Edinburgh: HMSO).
Maclure, S. (1988), *Education Re-formed* (London: Hodder and Stoughton).
Maychell, K. (1986), 'LEA implementation of the 1980 Act', in A. Stillman (ed.), *The Balancing Act of 1980. Parents, Politics and Education* (Slough: NFER), pp. 14–20.
McCormick, R. (ed.) (1982), *Calling Education to Account* (London: Heinemann).
McLaughlin, T. H. (1984), 'Parental rights and the religious upbringing of children', *Journal of Philosophy of Education*, vol. 18, no. 1, pp. 75–83.
Meredith, P. (1981), 'Executive discretion and choice of secondary school', *Public Law*, Spring, pp. 52–82.
Middleton, N. and Weitzman, S. (1976), *A Place for Everyone: a history of state education from the end of the 18th century to the 1970s* (London: Gollancz).
Midwinter, E. (1972), *Priority Education: an account of the Liverpool project* (London: Penguin).
Mill, J. S. ([1859] (1982)), *On Liberty* (London: Penguin).
Ministry of Education (1960), *Report of the Working Party on Assistance with the Cost of Boarding Education* Martin Report (London: HMSO).
Muskett, J. (1986), 'First impressions', *Times Educational Supplement*, 5 September.

National Society (Church of England) for Promoting Religious Education (1984), *A Future in Partnership* (London: National Society).
Niskanen, W. A. (1971), *Bureaucracy and Representative Government* (Chicago: Atherton).

Open University (1988), Course E325 *Managing Schools* (Milton Keynes: Open University Press).
Osborne, R. D., Cormack, R. J., Miller, R. L. (1987), *Education and Policy in Northern Ireland* (Belfast: Policy Research Institute).

Paine, T. ([1792] (1915)), *The Rights of Man* (New York: E. P. Dutton).
Passmore, B. (1984), 'Staff and parents condemn Green Paper', *Times Educational Supplement*, 1 June.
Pateman, T. (1988), 'No choice for the wicked', *Times Educational Supplement*, 19 February.
Pedley, R. (1956), *Comprehensive Education: a new approach* (London: Gollancz).
Pedley, R. (1963), *The Comprehensive School* (London: Penguin).
Petch, A. J. (1986), 'Parental choice at entry to primary school', *Research Papers in Education*, vol. 1, no. 1, pp. 26–47.
Petch, A. J. (1986a), 'Parents' reasons for choosing secondary schools', in A. Stillman (ed.), *The Balancing Act of 1980. Parents, Politics and Education* (Slough: NFER), pp. 28–35.
Petch, A. J. (1987), 'Early to school: under-age admissions in Scotland', *The Scottish Child*, vol. 1, no. 1, pp. 11–13.
Petch, A. J. (1988), 'Rezoning: an exercise in compromise', in L. Bondi and M. H. Matthews (eds), *Education and Society* (London: Routledge).
Pring, R. (1982), 'Privatisation', *Where*, no. 186, March, pp. 9–14.
Public Schools Commission (1968), *First Report of the Public Schools Commission* (London: HMSO).

Raab, G. M. and Adler, M. E. (1987), 'A tale of two cities: the impact of parental choice on admissions to primary schools in Edinburgh and Dundee', *Research Papers in Education*, vol. 2, no. 3, pp. 157–76.
Radice, G. (1986), *Equality and Quality: a Socialist Plan for Education*, Fabian Tract 514 (London: Fabian Society).
Rae, J. (1981), *The Public School Revolution* (London: Faber).
Ranson, S. (1990), *The Politics of Reorganizing Schools* (London: Unwin Hyman).
Ranson, S., Gray, J., Jesson, D. and Jones, B. (1986), 'Exams in context: values and power in educational accountability', in D. Nuttall (ed.), *Assessing Educational Achievement* (Lewes: Falmer), pp. 81–98.
Roebuck, S. (1986), *An Introduction to the Methodist Church and its Boarding Schools* (London: Board of Management for Methodist Boarding Schools).
Rogers, R. (1980), 'The myth of "independent" schools', *New Statesman*, vol. 99 (4 Jan) no. 2546, pp. 10–12.
Rowley, C. K. (1969), 'The political economy of British education', *Scottish Journal of Political Economy*, vol. 16, pp. 152–76.
Rutter, M., Maughan, B., Mortimore, P. and Ouston, J. (1979), *Fifteen Thousand Hours* (London: Open Books).

Salter, B. and Tapper, T. (1985), *Power and Policy in Education. The Case of Independent Schooling* (London: Falmer).
Seldon, A. (1986), *The Riddle of the Voucher* Hobart Paperback 21 (London: Institute of Economic Affairs).
Sharp, R. and Green, A. (1975), *Education and Social Control: a study in progressive primary education* (London: Routledge).
Shaw, J. (1980), 'Education and the individual: schooling for girls or mixed schooling – a mixed blessing?' in R. Deem (ed.), *Schooling for Women's Work* (London: Routledge), pp. 66–75.
Shaw, J. (1984), 'The politics of single-sex schools' in R. Deem (ed.), *Schooling for Women's Work* (London: Routledge), pp. 21–36.
Smith, A. ([1776] (1976)), *Wealth of Nations* R. H. Campbell and A. S. Skinner (eds) (Oxford: Clarendon Press).
Socialist Educational Association (1981), *The Dual System of Voluntary and County Schools* Discussion Document (Manchester: SEA).
Sockett, H. (ed.) (1980), *Accountability in the English Educational System* (London: Hodder & Stoughton).
Souper, P. C. and Kay, W. K. (1983), *The School Assembly Debate: 1942–1982* (Southampton: University of Southampton).
Steedman, J. (1983), *Examination Results in Mixed and Single Sex Schools; findings from the National Child Development Study* (Manchester: Equal Opportunities Commission).
Stillman, A. (ed.) (1986), *The Balancing Act of 1980. Parents, Politics and Education* (Slough: NFER).
Stillman, A. and Maychell, K. (1986), *Choosing Schools: parents, LEAs and the 1980 Education Act* (Windsor: NFER-Nelson).
Stoll, P. and O'Keeffe, D. (1989), *Officially Present* (London: Institute of Economic Affairs).
Stone, L. (1979), *The Family, Sex and Marriage in England, 1500–1800* (London: Penguin).
Straw, J. (1989), 'Parents squashed by the Tory steamroller', *Times Educational Supplement*, 11 September.
Sugarman, S. D. (1980), 'Family choice in education', *Oxford Review of Education*, vol. 6, no. 1, pp. 31–40.
Sutcliffe, J. (1989), 'Walsall announces closures', *Times Educational Supplement*, 1 September.
Swallow, J. (1984), 'Beauty reborn, or sleeping giant?', *Times Educational Supplement*, 15 June.

Tapper, T. and Salter, B. (1986), 'The Assisted Places Scheme: a policy evaluation', *Journal of Education Policy*, vol. 1, no. 4, pp. 315–330.
Tawney, R. H. ([1931] (1964)), *Equality* (London: Allen & Unwin).
Tweedie, J. W. (1986), 'Parental choice of school: legislating the balance', in A. Stillman (ed.) op. cit., pp. 3–11.
Tweedie, J. W. (1986a), 'Rights in social programmes; the case of parental choice of school', *Public Law*, Autumn, pp. 407–36.

Tweedie, J. W., Adler, M. E. and Petch, A. J. (1986), 'The rights and wrongs of education appeal committees'. Paper commissioned by and submitted to the Scottish Education Department.

University of Glasgow (1986), *Parental Choice of School in Scotland* (Glasgow: Department of Education, University of Glasgow).

Walford, G. (1984), 'Introduction: British Public Schools', in G. Walford (ed.), *British Public Schools: policy and practice* (London: Falmer), pp. 1–8.

Walford, G. (1986), *Life in Public Schools* (London: Methuen).

Walford, G. (1988), 'The Scottish Assisted Places Scheme: a comparative study of the origins, nature and practice of the APSs in Scotland, England and Wales', *Journal of Education Policy*, vol. 3, no. 2, pp. 137–53.

Wall, D. (1986), 'The Assisted Places Scheme and its operation in London Girls' Public Day School Trust Schools', MA dissertation, University of London Institute of Education.

Wallace, W. (1988), 'Why is our school so *schmutterdick*?', *Times Educational Supplement*, 5 February.

Warnock, M. (1975), 'The concept of equality in education', *Oxford Review of Education*, vol. 1, no. 1, pp. 3–8.

Webster, R. (1982), 'Education in Wales', in Cohen, Thomas and Manion, op. cit., pp. 203–14.

Weiner, G. and Arnot, M. (1987), *Gender and Education Bibliography* (Milton Keynes: Open University).

West, E. G. (1982), 'Education vouchers: evolution or revolution', *Economic Affairs*, vol. 3, no. 1, October.

Whitty, G., Fitz, J. and Edwards, T. (1989), 'Assisting whom? Benefits and costs of the Assisted Places scheme', in A. Hargreaves and D. Reynolds (eds), *Education Policies: controversies and critiques* (London: Falmer), pp. 138–60.

Wilby, P. (1988), 'How parental choice leads to social division', *The Independent*, 10 March.

Woods, P. (1979), *The Divided School* (London: Routledge).

Index

Index